MAKERS OF MODERN SOCIAL SCIENCE

# LEWIS A. COSER
## GENERAL EDITOR

ÉMILE DURKHEIM, by Robert A. Nisbet, *with selected essays,* S-118
GEORG SIMMEL, edited by Lewis A. Coser, S-119
PARETO & MOSCA, edited by James H. Meisel, S-122

FORTHCOMING VOLUMES

KARL MANNHEIM, edited by Paul Kecskemeti
MAX WEBER, edited by Dennis Wrong
SIGMUND FREUD, edited by Harold Lasswell
KARL MARX, edited by Thomas Bottomore

MAKERS OF MODERN SOCIAL SCIENCE
# GEORG SIMMEL

EDITED BY
## LEWIS A. COSER

A SPECTRUM BOOK

Prentice-Hall, Inc.
*Englewood Cliffs, New Jersey*

# CONTENTS

v

# GEORG SIMMEL

# GEORG SIMMEL

## LEWIS A. COSER

GEORG SIMMEL was born on March 1, 1858, in the very center of Berlin: on the corner of Leipzigerstrasse and Friedrichstrasse. This is a curious birthplace; it would correspond to the corner of New York's Broadway and Forty-second Street. It seems most fitting for Simmel: all his life he lived in the intersection of many conflicting currents, intensely affected by a multiplicity of intellectual and moral tendencies. He was a modern urban man, without roots in traditional folk culture, an alien in his native land. Like the stranger he described in one of his most brilliant essays, he was near and far at the same time, a "potential wanderer: although he [had] not moved on, he [had] not quite overcome the freedom of coming and going." [1] Many strains of German philosophy and thought converge in Simmel's work; yet, at the same time, he was quite distant from much of contemporary German culture. One of the major minds German social science produced around the turn of the century, he remains atypical, a perturbing and fascinating figure to his more organically rooted contemporaries.

Simmel was the youngest of seven children. While still very young, he lost his father, a prosperous Jewish businessman who had been converted to Christianity. A friend of the family, the owner of a music publishing house, was appointed the boy's guardian. Simmel's relation to his domineering mother was apparently rather distant. The youth seems not to have had roots in any secure family environment. A sense of marginality and insecurity came early to the young Simmel.

[1] *The Sociology of Georg Simmel,* translated and edited by Kurt H. Wolff (New York: The Free Press of Glencoe, Inc., 1950), p. 402.

After graduating from *Gymnasium,* Simmel studied history and philosophy at the University of Berlin with some of the most important academic figures of the day: the historians Mommsen, Treitschke, Sybel, and Droysen, the philosophers Harms and Zeller, the anthropologists Lazarus and Steinthal (who were the founders of *Völkerpsychologie*), and the psychologist Bastian. By the time he received his doctorate in philosophy (his thesis was entitled *The Nature of Matter According to Kant's Physical Monadology*), Simmel was familiar with vast fields of knowledge extending from history and philosophy to the social sciences. His whole career was marked by this catholicity of tastes and interests. His refusal to settle down to the cultivation of a narrow area of academic concern accounts for some of the vicissitudes and tragedies that beset his career. In this area, too, he insisted upon being a "stranger," resisting the manifold pressures of colleagues and superiors to limit himself to narrow scholarly work. He was involved in many inquiries, concerned with many fields, never willing to become part of any "gild," always maintaining his freedom to move on.

Simmel's philosophical writings—from the neo-Kantian positivism of his earlier years to the vitalism of his last work, which brought him near to Bergson—influenced Heidegger and Jaspers. His writings on aesthetics brought him the friendship of Rilke, Stefan George, and Rodin. His work in the philosophy and methodology of history parallels—and, in a number of cases, antecedes—the work of Dilthey, Rickert, and Windelband. His contribution to sociology is only one part of his work, though probably the most enduring. Turning away from the organicism of the evolutionist school as well as from the concern with concrete individual behavior of German *Geisteswissenschaft,* Simmel saw sociology as a study of individuals within groups and subgroups and within a network of social interaction. This vision was to form the basis for many later theories, but it was never fully elaborated by Simmel himself. His failure—or, perhaps, his refusal—to build his insights into a systematic body of theory is associated with the difficulties of his academic career.

Simmel started teaching at Berlin University in 1885, and soon became a very popular lecturer. His courses ranged from logic and the history of philosophy to ethics, social psychology, and sociology. He lectured on Darwin and on Kant, on Schopenhauer and on

Nietzsche. Often, he would survey new trends in sociology as well as in metaphysics during a single academic year. His lectures soon became leading intellectual events—not only for students but also for the cultural elite of Berlin. In spite of the fascination he called forth, however, Simmel's academic career was unfortunate, even tragic.

For fifteen years Simmel remained a *Privatdozent;* that is, an unpaid lecturer remunerated only by students' fees. In 1901, when he was forty-three, the academic authorities finally consented to grant him the rank of *Ausserordentlicher Professor,* a purely honorary title which did not allow him to take part in the affairs of the academic community. Even this failed to remove the stigma of the outsider. Only in 1914, at the age of fifty-six, was he called to Strasbourg as a full professor. Four years later he died of cancer.

The latent anti-Semitism which disfigured much of prewar academic life in Germany was one of the causes for the shabby treatment Simmel received from the academic powers that were, but it was not the only one. The breadth of Simmel's culture, his refusal to be restricted by any of the existing disciplines, perturbed many of the more settled spirits in the academic world. His originality, his sparkling intellect, and his ability to move with apparent effortlessness from one topic to another affronted colleagues and superiors who felt that only sustained application to specific problems suited the academic calling. How could one deal with a man who might, in one semester, offer a profound course on Kant's epistemology and, in the next, publish essays on the sociology of smell, on the sociology of meals, or on the sociology of coquetry and fashions?

Simmel was never tempted by the *esprit de système.* Whether from impatience or from sheer inability to concentrate for any length of time on a particular problem, he moved from one topic to the next, from one line of reasoning to another. He was like a bright-eyed youngster in a garden who moves from discovery to discovery, fascinated by the vivid color of this flower and the strange convolutions of that insect, filled with ever-renewed curiosity. Ortega y Gasset caught the spirit of the man when he compared him to a kind of philosophical squirrel, jumping from one nut to the other, scarcely bothering to nibble much at any of them, mainly concerned with performing his splendid exercises as he leaped from branch to branch, and rejoicing (or so it would seem) in the sheer gracefulness of his acrobatic leaps. One can perhaps understand, though not forgive, those professors who just did not know how to deal with academic squirrels, accustomed as they were to the deliberate movements of professorial pachyderms.

Simmel did not only produce brilliant *aperçus;* his contribution to the philosophy and methodology of history, to ethics and to general philosophy testify to the contrary. His work in sociology consists of a close scrutiny of many facets of social life. But in most of his essays Simmel imposes a heavy burden on the reader, leaving to him the task of discerning the steady concern with a central idea that lies beneath the flow of the writer's imagination. Reading Simmel for the first time is much like watching the burst of many-colored fireworks against a darkened sky. Nevertheless, sustained immersion in Simmel's writings reveals that there is a pattern beneath the apparent disorder.

### SIMMEL'S APPROACH TO SOCIOLOGY

Simmel's approach to sociology can best be understood as a self-conscious attempt to reject both the organicist realism of Comte and Spencer and the sociological nominalism and ideographic method of German *Geisteswissenschaft.*

When Simmel turned his attention to sociology, the field was generally conceived, in the manner of Comte and Spencer, as a queen of the social sciences. It was said to be the master science which could discover the laws governing all social developments. Moreover, sociology was most often characterized by the organicist approach so prominent in the works of Comte and Spencer in France and England and of Schäffle in Germany. This view stressed the fundamental continuity between nature and society. Societal change was seen as qualitatively similar to, although more complex than, biological process. Life was conceived as a great chain of being, stretching from the most simple natural phenomenon to the most highly differentiated social organism. Hence, the methods developed in the natural sciences, though they had to be adapted to the particular tasks of the social sciences, were considered not essentially different from those appropriate to the study of man in society.

This view of social life was vigorously opposed in the tradition of German scholarship which was formed in the school of idealistic philosophy. The German tradition viewed *Naturwissenschaft* and *Geisteswissenschaft* as qualitatively different. Natural laws could have no place in the study of human culture, which represented the realm of freedom. The methods appropriate to the study of human phenomena were ideographic rather than nomothetic. It behooved the student of human affairs to describe and record the unique events which marked human history; any attempt to establish nomothetic regularities in the sphere of human culture was expected to founder upon the rock of the autonomy of the human spirit. *Kultur* and *Natur* were essentially different realms of being.

Moreover, the proponents of the German tradition argued, sociology had no real object of study: the term *society* was but a rough label, convenient for certain purposes but devoid of substance or reality. There is no society, it was argued, outside or in addition to the individuals who compose it. Once these individuals and their historically located actions are investigated, nothing remains by way of subject matter for a science of society. Human freedom, the uniqueness and irreversibility of historical events, the fundamental disjunction between *Geist* and *Natur* all combined, so the German tradition asserted, to make attempts at founding a science of sociology a quixotic—nay! a scandalous—enterprise. Far from being queen of the sciences, sociology was not a science at all.

Simmel rejected both the organicist and the idealist schools. He did not see society as a thing or an organism, nor merely as a convenient label for something that did not have "real" existence. According to his view, society is, rather, an intricate web of multiple relations established among individuals in constant interaction with one another: "*Society* is merely the name for a number of individuals, connected by interaction." [2] The larger superindividual structures—the state, the clan, the family, the city, or the trade union —turn out to be but crystallizations of this interaction, even though they may attain autonomy and permanency and confront the individual as if they were alien powers. The major field of study for the student of society is, hence, *association* rather than society.

The grandiose claims of those who wish to make sociology the

[2] *Ibid.*, p. 10.

master science of everything human, Simmel argued, are self-defeating. *Qui trop embrasse, mal étreint.* Nothing can be gained by throwing together all phenomena heretofore studied by jurisprudence and philology, by political science and psychology, and labeling them *sociology*. By trying to embrace all phenomena which are in any way connected with human social life, by trying to create a science of everything human, one pursues a will-o'-the-wisp. There can be no such totalistic science, just as there is no "total" science of all matter. Science must study dimensions or aspects of phenomena rather than global totalities. Sociology cannot be the science of everything human; its legitimate subject matter lies, rather, in the description and analysis of particular forms of human interaction:

> Sociology asks what happens to men and by what rules they behave, not insofar as they unfold their understandable individual existences in their totalities, but insofar as they form groups and are determined by their group existence because of interaction.[3]

Although all human behavior is individual behavior, much of it can be explained in terms of the individual's group affiliation and in terms of the constraints imposed upon him by particular forms of interaction.

Though Simmel considered the larger institutionalized structures a legitimate field of sociological inquiry, he preferred to restrict most of his work to an investigation of what he called "interactions among the atoms of society." [4] He limited his concern, in the main, to those fundamental patterns of interaction among individuals which underlie the larger social formations. The method he advocated and practiced focused attention upon the perennial and limited number of *forms* which such interaction might take.

FORMAL SOCIOLOGY

Sociology, as conceived by Simmel, did not pretend to usurp the subject matter of economics, ethics, psychology, or historiography; rather, it concentrated on the forms of interaction that underlie political, economic, religious, and sexual behavior. In Simmel's

[3] *Ibid.,* p. 11.
[4] *Ibid.,* p. 10.

perspective a host of otherwise distinct human phenomena might be properly understood by reference to the same formal concept. To be sure, the student of warfare and the student of marriage investigate qualitatively different subject matters, yet the sociologist might be able to discern in martial and marital conflict essentially similar interactive forms. Though there is but little concrete similarity between the behavior displayed at the court of Louis XIV and that displayed in the main offices of an American corporation, a study of the forms of subordination and superordination in each may reveal underlying patterns common to both. On a concrete and descriptive level, there would seem little connection between, say, the early psychoanalytic movement in Vienna and the Trotskyist movement, but attention to typical forms of interaction among the members of these groups reveals that both are importantly shaped by the fact that they have the structural features of the sect.

Simmel's insistence on the forms of interaction as the peculiar domain for sociological inquiry was his decisive response to those historians and other representatives of the humanities who denied that a science of society could ever come to grips with the novelty, the irreversibility, and the uniqueness of historical phenomena. To be sure, Simmel argued, particular historical events are unique: the murder of Caesar, the accession of Henry VIII, the defeat of Napoleon at Waterloo are all events located at a particular moment in time and possessed of a nonrecurrent significance. Yet, if one looks at history through the peculiar lenses of the sociologist, one need not concern himself with the uniqueness of these events but, rather, with their underlying uniformities. The sociologist does not contribute to knowledge about the individual actions of a King John, or a King Louis, or a King Henry. But he can illuminate the ways in which all of them were constrained in their actions by the institution of kingship. The sociologist is not concerned with King *John* but, rather, with *King* John. And, at a more microscopic level, he might not even be concerned with the institution of kingship but, rather, with the processes of conflict and cooperation, of subordination and superordination, of centralization and decentralization which constitute, so to speak, the building blocks upon which the larger institutional structure is erected. In this way, Simmel wanted to build a geometry of social life:

Geometric abstraction investigates only the spatial forms of bodies, although empirically these forms are given merely as the forms of some material content. Similarly, if society is conceived as interaction among individuals, the description of the forms of this interaction is the task of the science of society in its strictest and most essential sense.[5]

Simmel's distinction between the form and the content of social phenomena is not always as clear as might be desired. As other contributions to this volume will show in more detail, Simmel gave somewhat variant definitions of these concepts, and his treatment of particular topics reveals some obvious inconsistencies. What is considered form in one essay may be considered content in another. The essence of his thought, nevertheless, is clear. Formal sociology isolates form from the heterogeneity of content, and purpose from the variety of interests—be they material or ideal—which actuate human beings. It attempts to show that, however diverse the interests and purposes which give rise to specific associations among men, the forms in which these interest and purposes are realized may yet be identical. Thus, both war and profit-making involve cooperation. Inversely, identical interests and purposes may crystallize into different forms. Economic interests may be realized in competition as well as in planned cooperation, and aggressive drives may be satisfied in a variety of forms of conflict.

In formal analysis, certain features of concrete phenomena, which are not readily observable unless such a perspective is applied to them, are extracted from reality. Once this has been successfully accomplished, it becomes possible to compare phenomena which may be radically different in concrete content yet essentially similar in structural arrangement. On this point Simmel is often misunderstood: he was not asserting that forms have a separate and distinct existence, but that they inhere in content and can have no separate reality. Simmel was far from a Platonic view of essences. He stressed that concrete phenomena could be studied from a variety of perspectives and that analysis of the limited number of forms which could be extracted from the bewildering multiplicity of social contents might contribute insights into social life denied to those who would be content with descriptions of the concrete.

The term *form*, being freighted with a great deal of philosophical

[5] *Ibid.*, pp. 21-22.

ballast, some of it of a rather dubious nature, was perhaps not a very happy one. It may well be that it has tended to frighten away certain modern sociologists intent on exorcising any metaphysical ghosts that might interfere with the building of a scientific sociology. One cannot but feel that had Simmel used the term *social structure*—which, in a sense, is quite near to his use of *form*—he would have encountered less resistance. As F. H. Tenbruck makes clear in his fine essay included here, such modern sociological terms as *status*, *role, norms*, and *expectations* as elements of social structure are very near to the formal conceptualizations that Simmel employed. (It might be noted that Simmel uses the notion of *role* throughout his work in a quite "modern" way, anteceding Ralph Linton's definition of the concept by many years.)

Furthermore, much of the building of modern sociological theory proceeds precisely with the help of the perspective that Simmel has advocated. For example, in his reanalysis of some of the data of *The American Soldier*,[6] Merton, when accounting for the behavior of "green" troops in terms of their relationships with seasoned troops in different structural contexts, uses this perspective to account more generally for social situations in which newcomers are involved in interaction with oldtimers. By abstracting from the concrete content of army life, Merton accounts for certain aspects of the behavior of newcomers—from immigrants to college freshmen—in relation to pre-existing groups. It follows that the newcomer-oldtimer relationship, or the newcomer as a social type, can now be understood as a particular form that might profitably be studied through a process of abstraction from the various concrete social situations that are being observed. It is through such abstraction from concrete social content that the building of a theory becomes possible.

To Simmel, the forms found in social reality are never pure; every social phenomenon contains a multiplicity of formal processes. Co-operation and conflict, subordination and superordination, intimacy and distance—all may be operative in a concrete marital relationship or in a bureaucratic structure. In concrete phenomena, moreover, the presence of a multiplicity of forms leads to their interference

---

[6] Robert K. Merton and Alice S. Rossi, "Contributions to the Theory of Reference Group Behavior," in Robert K. Merton, *Social Theory and Social Structure,* rev. ed. (New York: The Free Press of Glencoe, Inc., 1957), pp. 225-80.

with one another, so that none of them can ever be realized in purity. There is no "pure" conflict in social life, just as there is no "pure" cooperation. "Pure" forms are constructs—typical relationships never to be completely realized. Here Simmel comes very near to Weber's notion of the *ideal-type*. Simmel's forms are not generalizations about aspects of reality, but they tend to heighten or to exaggerate "so as to bring out configurations and relations which underlie reality but are not factually actualized in it." [7] Just as the art historian speaks of "Gothic" or "baroque" style, even though no known work of architecture exhibits all the elements of either style in all their purity, so may the sociologist construct a "pure" type or form of social conflict even though no empirically known process fully embodies it. Just as Weber's ideal-type may be conceived as a measuring rod to help calculate the distance between a concrete phenomenon and the type, so a Simmelian form—say, the typical combination of nearness and distance that marks the relation of "the stranger" from the surrounding world—may help to gauge the degree of "strangerness" inherent in the specific historical circumstances of, say, Jews or other pariah peoples.

THE DIALECTICAL METHOD IN SIMMEL'S SOCIOLOGY

Although in many respects Simmel's sociology is not as far from the preoccupations of modern sociology as his somewhat awkward terminology might indicate, there is nonetheless one very important area in which he departs from at least one strain of modern sociological tradition. Much contemporary sociological theory tends to accept what Dennis Wrong has recently called an "oversocialized conception of man," a conception in which individuals are seen almost exclusively in terms of their roles and their responses to the normative requirements of social systems. In contrast, Simmel stresses throughout his work the dialectical tension between the individual and society. Simmel see individuals as products of society, as links in the societal process, yet

> . . . the total content of life, even though it may be fully accounted for in terms of social antecedents and interactions, must yet be looked

[7] Tenbruck, this volume.

at at the same time under the aspect of singularity, as oriented toward the experience of the individual.[8]

According to Simmel, the socialized individual always remains in a dual relation toward society: he is incorporated within it and yet stands against it. The individual is, at the same time, within and outside society—for it and for himself:

> [Social man] is not partially social and partially individual; rather, his existence is shaped by a fundamental unity, which cannot be accounted for in any other way than through the synthesis or coincidence of two logically contradictory determinations: man is both social link and being for himself, both product of society and life from an autonomous center. . . ." [9]

The individual is determined, yet determining; acted upon, yet self-actuating.

The insistence on the pervasive dialectic of the relation between individual and society, the insistence that incorporation into the network of social relations is the ineluctable fate of human life, while it is also an obstacle to self-actualization, informs all of Simmel's sociological thought. Society allows the emergence of individuality and autonomy, but it also impedes it. The forms of social life impress themselves upon each individual and allow him to become specifically human. At the same time, they also imprison and stultify the human personality. Only in and through institutional forms can man attain freedom, yet his freedom is forever endangered by these very institutional forms.

Simmel's sociology is throughout informed by the dialectic approach which characterizes his treatment of individual and society. In this respect also he would find himself at variance with certain tendencies in current sociological theory. For instance, Simmel would have rejected any attempt to understand societies by way of models emphasizing exclusively those processes making for harmony, consensus, and balance among component individuals and groups. To Simmel, sociation always involves harmony *and* conflict, attraction *and* repulsion, love *and* hatred. He saw human relations as characterized by ambivalence; precisely those who are connected in

[8] Georg Simmel, *Soziologie* (Leipzig: Duncker und Humblot, 1908), p. 40.
[9] *Ibid.*, p. 41.

intimate relations are likely to harbor for one another not only positive but also negative sentiments.

An entirely harmonious group, Simmel argued, could not exist empirically. It would not partake of any kind of life process; it would be incapable of change and development. Any social relationship needs attractive and repulsive forces, harmony and disharmony, in order to attain a specific form. Moreover, Simmel stressed, it was naïve to view those forces making for conflict as negative and those making for consensus as positive. On the contrary, sociation is always the resultant of both categories of interaction; both are positive ingredients, structuring all relationships and giving them enduring form.

Simmel tended to differentiate sharply between social appearances and social realities. Thus, although a given conflictive relationship might be considered wholly negative by participants or by outside observers, it could nevertheless be shown to have latent positive functions. Only a withdrawal from a relationship could be considered wholly negative; a conflictive relationship—though it might be considered painful by one or more participants—nevertheless remains a relationship, tying them to the social fabric. It is essential to recognize, Simmel argued, that social conflict necessarily involves reciprocal action and is, hence, based on reciprocity rather than unilateral imposition. Conflict might often bind parties which might otherwise withdraw. It might serve as a safety valve for negative attitudes and feelings, making further relationships possible. For example, conflict might lead to a strengthening of the position of one or more parties to the relationship, increasing their dignity and self-esteem through self-assertion. Thus, conflict might produce new ties among the participants, strengthening their existing bonds or establishing new ones. In this sense, conflict might be considered a creative force rather than a destructive one.

Simmel never dreamed of a frictionless universe, of a society from which clashes and contentions among individuals and groups would be forever banned. For him, conflict is the very essence of social life, an ineradicable component of social living. The good society —far from conflict-free—is, on the contrary, "sewn together" by a variety of crisscrossing conflicts among its component parts.[10]

[10] Cf. Georg Simmel, *Conflict and the Web of Group Affiliations,* translated

In Simmel's view, peace and feud, conflict and order, are correlative. Both the cementing and the breaking of custom constitute part of the eternal dialectic of social life. It would, hence, be ill-advised to distinguish a sociology of order from one of disorder, a model of harmony from one of conflict. These are not distinct realities but only differing formal aspects of one reality. Simmel would have agreed with Charles Horton Cooley that "conflict and cooperation are not separable things, but phases of one process which always involves something of both." [11]

Throughout his work, Simmel considered the individual's social actions not in themselves but in relation to those of other individuals and to particular structures or processes. He is a resolutely functionalist thinker. In his famous chapter on "Superordination and Subordination," for example, he shows that domination does not consist in the unilateral imposition of the superordinate's will upon the subordinate but, rather, that it involves reciprocal action. What appears to be the imposition of absolute influence on the one hand, and the acquiescence to absolute influence on the other, is deceptive. Influence "conceals an interaction, an exchange . . . , which transforms the pure one-sidedness of superordination and subordination into a *sociological* form." [12] Thus the superordinate's action cannot be understood without reference to the subordinate, and vice versa. Ego's action can only be analyzed by reference to Alter's reaction; the two are part of a system of interaction which constrains both. Attempts to analyze social action without reference to the reactions which it calls forth and which condition further action would have been rejected by Simmel as examples of what he called *the fallacy of separateness*.

Moreover, he does not rest his case after demonstrating that domination is a form of interaction. He proceeds to show in considerable detail the particular ways in which various types of group structure are associated with different forms of subordination and superordination—distinguishing, for example, between gradation

by Kurt H. Wolff and Reinhard Bendix (New York: The Free Press of Glencoe, Inc., 1955). See also Lewis A. Coser, *The Functions of Social Conflict* (New York: The Free Press of Glencoe, Inc., 1956).

[11] Charles H. Cooley, *Social Process* (New York: Charles Scribner's Sons, 1918), p. 39.

[12] *The Sociology of Georg Simmel, op. cit.*, p. 186.

and leveling. If a number of individuals are equally subject to one individual, he argued, they are themselves equal. Such "negative democratization," to use Karl Mannheim's term, favors and is favored by despotic rulers. Despots try to level their subjects and, conversely, highly developed leveling easily leads to despotism. Strong intermediate gradations among a ruler's subjects, on the other hand, tend to cushion his impact on them and thus weaken his hold over them. Intermediate powers, though they may increase inequalities in the subject population, shield the individual from the direct powers of the ruler. A pyramidal form of social gradation, whether it develops under the plan of the ruler or results from the usurpation of some of his power by subordinates, gives every one of its elements a position both lower and higher than the next rungs in the hierarchy. In this way, each level—except the very highest and the very lowest—is subordinate to the authorities above and, at the same time, is superordinate to the rungs beneath. Dependence on some persons is compensated by authority over others.

### THE SIGNIFICANCE OF NUMBERS FOR SOCIAL LIFE

Simmel's emphasis on the structural determinants of social action is perhaps best exemplified in his seminal essay, "Quantitative Aspects of the Group." [13] Here Simmel comes nearest to realizing his aim to write a grammar of social life by considering one of the most abstract characteristics of a group: the mere number of its participants. He examines forms of group process and structural arrangement insofar as these derive from sheer quantitative relationships.

A dyadic relationship, Simmel argues, differs qualitatively from all other types of group in that each of the two participants is confronted by only one other and not by a collectivity. Because this type of group depends only on two participants, the withdrawal of one would destroy the whole: "In the dyad, the sociological process remains, in principle, within personal interdependence and does not result in a structure that grows beyond its elements." [14]

Hence the dyad does not attain that superpersonal life which, in all other groups, creates among its members a sense of dependence

[13] *Ibid.*, pp. 87-177.
[14] *Ibid.*, p. 126.

and constraint. Yet the very lack of superpersonal structure also entails intense absorption of the participants in their dyadic relationship. The dependence of the whole on each partner is obvious; in all other groups duties and responsibilities can be delegated, but not in the dyad, where each participant is immediately and directly responsible for any collective action. Because each partner in the dyad deals with only one other individual, who forms a unit with him, neither of the two can deny responsibility by shifting it to the group; neither can hold the group responsible for what he has done or failed to do.

When a dyad is transformed into a triad, the apparently insignificant fact that one member has been added actually brings about a major qualitative change. In the triad, as in all associations involving more than two persons, the individual participant is confronted with the possibility of being outvoted by a majority.

The triad is the simplest structure in which the group as a whole can achieve domination over its component members; it provides a social framework which allows the constraining of individual participants for collective purposes. The dyad relies on immediate reciprocity, but the triad can impose its will upon one member through the formation of a coalition between the two others. Thus, the triad exhibits in its simplest form the sociological drama which, for Simmel, informs all social life: the dialectic of freedom and constraint, of autonomy and heteronomy.

When a third member enters a dyadic group, a variety of processes which previously could not take place becomes possible. Simmel singled out three of these processes, although others might be conceivable. A third member may play the role of mediator vis-à-vis the other two, helping—through his own impartiality—to moderate passions that threaten to tear the group apart. He may, alternately, act as a *tertius gaudens,* seeking to profit from disagreement between the other two and to turn it to his own advantage. Finally, through a strategy of *divide et impera,* he may intentionally create conflicts between the other two in order to attain a dominant position or other gains.

This brief outline of the three types of strategy open to the third participant can hardly suggest the richness of Simmel's thought in this analysis. He offers a great variety of examples, deliberately

comparing intimate human involvements such as the competition
of two men for one woman with such large-scale events as the European balance of power and the formations of coalitions among
political parties. He compares the ways in which Rome, after sub-
jugating Greece, dealt with Athens and Sparta with the strategy of
a mother-in-law who confronts a newly married couple. In both
cases, the third member can mediate between the other two, or
aggravate the conflict between them for his own benefit.

It is a virtuoso performance. And one cannot but be convinced
that it constitutes one of the most persuasive demonstrations of the
power of sociological analysis. Simmel reveals the sterility of psychological reductionism by demonstrating how the apparently peripheral fact that a third member has been added to a group of two
opens up possibilities for actions and processes that could not otherwise have come into existence. He thereby underlines the new properties that emerge from the forms of association among individuals.
The triadic group form provides new avenues of social action at
the same time that it restricts other opportunities—such as the expression of individuality—which were available in the dyadic
group.

Simmel shows that the triad is the simplest of the group forms
which can achieve a superindividual existence. Yet he does not rest
his analysis of numbers at this point. Although it is not possible to
demonstrate that each addition of new members would produce a
distinct sociological entity, he shows that there is a crucial difference between small groups and larger ones.

In small groups, members typically have a chance to interact directly with one another; once the group exceeds a relatively limited
size, such interaction must be mediated through formal arrangements. In order to come to grips with the increasing complexity of
relationships among large numbers of individuals, the group must
create special organs to help the patterning of interactions among
its members. Thus, no large group can function without the invention of offices, the differentiation of status positions, and the delegation of tasks and responsibilities. This is why larger groups must
be societies of unequals: in order to maintain themselves, they must
be structurally differentiated. But this means that the larger group
"gains its unity, which finds expression in the group organs and in

political notions and ideals, only at the price of a great distance between all of these structures and the individual." [15]

The smaller the group, the greater the involvement of its members, for interaction among a few tends to be more intense than interaction among many, if only because of the greater frequency of contact among them. Inversely, the larger the group, the weaker the participation of its members and the higher the chances that they will be involved with only a segment of their personalities rather than as whole human beings. The larger group fragments involvement; it demands less of its members, yet it also creates "objective" structures that confront individuals with superpersonal powers:

> For it is this large number which paralyzes the individual element and which causes the general element to emerge at such a distance from it that it seems that it could exist by itself, without any individuals, to whom in fact it often enough is antagonistic.[16]

The larger group, by creating a greater distance among its members, liberates the individual from close control and scrutiny even as, through its formal arrangements, it confronts the individual with a distant and alien power. In the dyad, the immediacy of the *we* is not yet marred by the intrusion of structural constraints. In the triad, the two may constrain the third member of the group and force their will upon him. In the small group, however, the coalitions and majorities that act to constrain individual action are mitigated by the immediacy of participation. In the large group, on the other hand, the group organs constrain the individual through their "objective" powers, even as they allow freedom from the group through segmental rather than total involvement.

Simmel's discussion of the differences between small groups and large groups—between the intensity of involvement among individuals in the primary group and the distance, aloofness, and segmentation of individuals in larger groups—reveals his general dialectic approach to the relation between individual freedom and group structure. His minute sociological analysis is part of his general philosophical view of the drift of modern history. Like Tönnies

[15] *Ibid.*, p. 96.
[16] *Ibid.*, p. 96.

and Durkheim, Simmel theorizes about types and properties of group relations and social solidarities as part of a more general endeavor to assess and evaluate the major trends of historical development and to elaborate a diagnosis of his time.

### SIMMEL'S AMBIVALENT VIEW OF MODERN CULTURE

Nothing, perhaps, reveals as clearly Simmel's profoundly ambivalent attitude toward contemporary culture and society as his view of the drift of modern history. This view is a compound of the apparently contradictory assessments of liberal progressivism and of cultural pessimism, as in the writings of Herbert Spencer, on the one hand, and those of German idealism since the days of Schiller or Nietzsche, on the other.

The trend of modern history appears to Simmel as a progressive liberation of the individual from the bonds of exclusive attachment and personal dependencies even as it reveals the increasing domination of man by cultural products of his own creation. Man in premodern societies, Simmel argued, typically lived in a very limited number of relatively small social circles. Such circles—whether they were kinship groups, gilds, or towns and villages—tightly surrounded the individual and held him firmly in their grip. The total personality of the individual was immersed in group life. Thus, medieval organizational forms "occupied the whole man[;] they did not only serve an objectively determined purpose, but were rather a form of unification englobing the total person of those who had gathered together in the pursuit of that purpose." [17] Association in premodern societies was not functionally specific but, rather, bound the individual through diffuse dependencies and loyalties. Moreover, subordination in premodern society typically involved domination over the entire personality of the subordinate. The lord of the manor was not only the political overlord of the serf; he also dominated the total person of the serf economically, juridically, and socially. Dependence, in premodern societies, was all-encompassing.

In these societies, the individuals were organized, as it were, in a number of concentric circles which formed a hierarchical continuum. A man might have been a member of a gild while this

---

[17] *Soziologie, op. cit.,* p. 419.

gild, in turn, might have been part of a wider confederation of gilds. A burgher may have been a citizen of a particular town, while this town may have belonged to a federation of towns—say, the *Hanse*. An individual did not become a member of a higher social unit as an individual but, rather, as a member of a unit in a lower order of the hierarchy. The individual could not directly join the larger social circle but, rather, became involved in it by virtue of membership in a smaller one. A primitive tribe does not consist of individual members but rather of clans, lineages, or other groupings in which individuals participate directly.

The principle of organization in the modern world is fundamentally different: an individual is a member of many circles, each of which involves and controls only a part of his personality: "The number of different circles in which individuals move, is one of the indices of cultural development." [18] Modern man participates segmentally in a multiplicity of functionally specific circles, none of which can encompass his total personality or that of any of its members. He belongs to kinship groups, to occupational groupings, and to various other associations. This means that each individual occupies a distinct position in the intersection of many circles. Because there are many possible combinations of membership, each individual has a unique location in the social sphere. Though one may share membership with other individuals in one or several circles, he is unlikely to be located at exactly the same intersection as anyone else.

Human personality is transformed when membership in a single circle is replaced by a social position at the intersection of a great number of such circles. The personality is now highly segmented through participation in many circles. In premodern societies, for example, locality or kinship determined religious affiliation. In such societies one could not coexist with men who did not share his religious beliefs, for the religious community coincided with the territorial or kinship community. In the modern world, on the other hand, these allegiances are separated. A man may not share the religious beliefs of his neighbors, yet he may be tied to them by other bonds. It does not follow that religion therefore looses its force; it only becomes more specific. Religious concerns are differentiated

[18] *Ibid.*, p. 411.

from other concerns and hence become more individualized; they do not overlap a person's kinship or neighborhood ties.

Multifaceted involvement in a variety of circles contributes to increased self-consciousness. As the individual escapes the domination of the small circle which imprisons his personality within its confines, he becomes conscious of a sense of liberation. The segmentation of group involvement brings about a sense of uniqueness and of freedom. The intersection of social circles is the precondition for the emergence of individualism. Not only do men become more unlike one another, they are also afforded the opportunity to move without effort in different social contexts.

Moreover, the forms of subordination and superordination assume a novel character in the modern world. No longer can the individual be totally dominated by others; whatever domination continues to exist is functionally specific and limited to a particular time and place. The modern employer cannot dominate the entire personalities of the workers in his factory; his power over them is limited to a specifically economic context and a specified number of hours. Once the workers leave the factory gates, they are "free" to take part in other types of social relations in other social circles. Although they may be subordinate in some of these relations, they may well be superordinate in others, thus compensating for their inferiority in one area by superiority in another.

This sketch should have served to show how Simmel, in his original manner, is retracing the liberal view of historical patterns which could be found in such otherwise diverse thinkers as Spencer, Durkheim, or Maine. Differentiation, in this view, leads from homogeneity to heterogeneity, from uniformity to individualization, from absorption in the predictable routines of a small world of tradition to participation in a wider world of multifaceted involvements and open possibilities. The drift of Western history leads from status to contract, from mechanical solidarity to organic solidarity, from societies in which custom is so rigid that it prevents the emergence of individuality to those in which the multiplicity of involvements and contacts allows the eclosion of uniqueness and individual autonomy.

Yet this is only one of the two perspectives through which Simmel considers the past and present cultural situation. Another view contained in many of his writings owes more to Marx and German cultural pessimism then to the optimism of British and French progressive thought. From this perspective, Simmel writes of the ineradicable dualism which marks the relation between any individual subject and objective cultural values. The individual can attain cultivation only by appropriating the cultural values which surround him. Yet these values at any particular moment threaten to engulf and to subjugate the individual. More specifically, the division of labor, while it marks the origin of a differentiated cultural life, also subjugates and enslaves the individual.

The human mind creates a variety of products which, once created, have an existence independent of their creator as well as of those who receive or reject them. Hence the individual is perpetually confronted with a world of cultural objects, from religion to technology, from customs to science, which—though internalized—remain alien powers. They attain a fixed and coagulated form and thus must appear as "otherness" to the individual. Hence, there is a perennial contradiction "between subjective life, which is restless but limited and time-bound, and its contents which, once created, are immovable but timelessly valid." [19]

The individual needs art and science, religion and law, technique and legal norm in order to attain autonomy and to realize his own value. He needs to internalize these cultural values, making them part of himself. Individual excellence can be attained only through absorption of external values. And yet the fetishistic character which Marx attributed to the economic realm in the epoch of commodity production constitutes only a special case of the general fate of cultural contents. These contents are always—particularly in more developed cultural epochs—involved in a peculiar paradox: they have been created by subjects and they were intended for subjects, but they attain an objective form, and follow an immanent logic of development, becoming alienated from their origin as well as from their purpose.[20]

Modern man especially seems surrounded by a world of objects which are no longer in tune with human needs but which, instead,

[19] Georg Simmel, "Der Begriff und die Tragödie der Kultur," in *Philosophische Kultur* (Potsdam: Gustav Kiepenheuer Verlag, 1923), p. 236.
[20] *Ibid.*, p. 260.

constrain and dominate his needs and desires. Technology creates "unnecessary" products to fill "artificial" wants; science creates "unnecessary" knowledge—knowledge which is of no particular value but is simply the by-product of the autonomous expansion of scientific activities.

As a result of these trends, modern man finds himself in a deeply problematical situation: he is surrounded by a multiplicity of cultural elements which, though they are not meaningless to him, are not fundamentally meaningful either. They oppress the individual because he cannot fully assimilate them, yet he cannot reject them because they belong—at least potentially—to the sphere of his own cultural development:[21] "The cultural objects become more and more linked to each other in a self-contained world which has increasingly fewer contacts with the subjective psyche and its desires and sensibilities." [22] Simmel, like Marx, exemplifies this process by reference to the division of labor. Once this division is highly developed,

> . . . the perfection of the product is attained at the cost of the development of the producer. The increase in physical and psychical energies and skills which accompanies one-sided activities does hardly benefit the total personality; in fact it often leads to atrophy because it sucks away those forces that are necessary for the harmonious development of the full personality.[23]

The division of labor severs the creator from the creation so that the latter attains an autonomy of its own. This process of reification of the cultural products—accentuated, though not originated, by the division of labor—makes for increasing alienation between the subject and its products. The producer can no longer find himself within his product; rather, he loses himself in it.

The cultural universe is made by men, yet each individual perceives it as a world he never made. Thus, progress in the development of objective cultural products leads to a progressive impoverishment of the creating individuals. Those who are the producers

[21] *Ibid.*, p. 264.
[22] Georg Simmel, *Philosophie des Geldes* (Leipzig: Duncker und Humblot, 1900), p. 492.
[23] *Ibid.*, p. 484.

or consumers of objective culture tend to atrophy in their individual capacities even as they depend on it for their own cultivation.

Although committed with one facet of his *Weltanschauung* to the progressive liberal vision of those French and English thinkers who influenced him deeply, Simmel is yet equally bound to a tragic vision of culture. He combines in an original, though not fully resolved, way the uncomplicated evolutionary faith in the perfectibility of man of a Condorcet or a Spencer with the metaphysical pathos of a Schiller or a Nietzsche. Unable to relinquish the vision of a progressive liberation of the individual from the bonds of tradition and subjugation, Simmel yet foretells—with a sense of impending doom—"a cage of the future" (to use Weber's term), in which individuals will be frozen into societal functions and in which the price of the objective perfection of the world will be the atrophy of the human soul.

SIMMEL'S INFLUENCE

It was not granted to Simmel to solve the tensions and contradictions with which he grappled throughout his life. He made a last attempt, under the shadow of death, to develop a comprehensive vitalistic philosophy.[24] In this last book he celebrated the ultimate victory of life over form, of movement over *stasis*. Simmel now conceived of life as "an irreversible current in which each moment dissolves into the next." [25] This did not serve, however, to unify his philosophy, nor was it an answer to his many conflicting tendencies.[26]

Because he was unable to develop a consistent sociological or philosophical system, it is not altogether surprising that Simmel did not succeed in creating a "school," or that he left few direct disciples. Simmel, with his accustomed lucidity and self-consciousness, wrote in his diary not long before his death:

[24] Georg Simmel, *Lebensanschauung: Vier metaphysische Kapitel* (Munich and Leipzig: Duncker und Humblot, 1918).

[25] Georg Simmel, *Fragmente und Aufsätze* (Munich: Drei Masken Verlag, 1923), p. 185.

[26] Heinrich Rickert's cool neo-Kantian reply, "Movement is a relational concept and presupposes an unmoved in relation to which something is moving," constitutes, or so it would seem, a decisive riposte to such vitalistic metaphysics. See Heinrich Rickert, *Die Philosophie des Lebens,* 2nd ed. (Tübingen: J. C. B. Mohr [Paul Siebeck], 1922), p. 72.

I know that I shall die without intellectual heirs—and that is as it should be. My legacy will be, as it were in cash, distributed to many heirs, each transforming his part into use conformed to *his* nature: a use which will reveal no longer its indebtness to this heritage.[27]

This is, indeed, what happened. Simmel's influence on the further development of sociology, acknowledged or not, has been diffuse; yet it has been pervasive even during those periods in which his fame seemed to have been in eclipse.

Robert K. Merton once called Simmel "that man of innumerable seminal ideas." [28] This is why it would require a stout volume to trace his influence in numberless areas of sociological inquiry.

The modern critique of mass culture and mass society owes a huge, though often unacknowledged, debt to Simmel. These critiques, although they pride themselves on capturing the novelty of recent American experience, retrace the steps of arguments developed by Simmel half a century ago. Similarly, though much current discussion of alienation and anomie is linked to the twin influences of Marx and Durkheim, Simmel's contribution to these discussions has been far from negligible. As Raymond Aron and others have pointed out, the author of *The Stranger* is among the foremost commentators on the isolation, rootlessness, and malleability of modern industrial man. *The Lonely Crowd* was hardly discovered in 1950; its outlines can be traced in many an essay by Simmel.

Simmel's influence was not limited to those social analysts and critics who attempted to trace the major lines of contemporary man's predicament; it was just as pronounced on more sober, less crisis-oriented social theorists and social researchers. His work gave a major impetus to the pioneers of urban sociology in the United States. More particularly, the delineation of urban personalities and of the peculiar life-styles of urban man which are to be found in the works of Robert Park or Louis Wirth can, in large measure, be traced to Simmel, especially to his essay on "The Metropolis and Mental Life." Simmel's peculiar intimacy with the problems of social distance enabled him to capture key characteristics of the life-styles of metropolitan man that were directly echoed in the work of the urban sociologists of the Chicago school.

[27] Georg Simmel, "Nachgelassenes Tagebuch," in *Logos*, VII (1919), 121.
[28] Merton, *op. cit.*, p. 404.

Simmel's formal method, by which he attempts to transcend concrete events by reference to an abstract formal category encompassing manifold concrete objects, was taken up by Leopold von Wiese and the Cologne school of German sociology in the interwar years, although in this attempt to systematize Simmel's thought much of the sparkle and brilliance of his approach was lost. Formal sociology became formalistic sociology and the passion for cataloging and codifying social processes led to higher sociological bookkeeping rather than to fruitful investigation. In the United States, in contrast, no systematic effort was made to follow up Simmel's formal sociology. Here he has instead inspired much of the sociography and sociology of both natural and artificial (i.e., laboratory), groups.[29] In the field of experimental small-group research, Simmel's impact looms large. This field, which—until recently—has perhaps been more conspicuous for the rigor of its methods than for the sophistication of its theories, has utilized or tested only few prior theoretical formulations. But among these few those of Simmel stand out, as testified by a whole series of papers on coalition formation, on dyads, and on triads. Theodore Mills' paper in this volume will serve as an example.

The most systematic and comprehensive classification of group structures and group properties in modern sociological literature, Robert K. Merton's *Contributions to the Theory of Reference Group Behavior* and his *Continuities in the Theory of Reference Groups and Social Structure,* owes much to Simmel. Merton has acknowledged that "Simmel's writings were, beyond comparison, the most fruitful for the purpose" of gathering sociological materials to establish a list of group properties.[30] Although Simmel's influence on the microsociology of social groups is clearly acknowledged and fairly conspicuous, his influence on macrosociological theorizing and on social-system theory is perhaps less easily traceable. Yet theories of social conflict have been clearly marked by Simmel. This

[29] For earlier work in these areas, cf. Logan Wilson, "Sociology of Groups," in Georges Gurvitch and Wilbert C. Moore (eds.), *Twentieth Century Sociology* (New York: The Philosophical Library, Inc., 1945), pp. 139-71. For later works, see any of the many collections and codifications of small-group research: e.g., A. Paul Hare, *et al., Small Groups: Studies in Social Interaction* (New York: Alfred A. Knopf, Inc., 1955).

[30] Merton, *op. cit.,* p. 310.

writer's *The Functions of Social Conflict*[31] constituted, in large part, an effort to specify, systematize, and extend Simmel's insights into the subject. In other areas of structural-functional or social-system theory, Simmel's influence is somewhat less evident. Talcott Parsons, for example, has made few references to Simmel's work, though Merton and Kingsley Davis have often acknowledged their debt to him. One thing is fairly certain: the concept of *social role,* so central to much contemporary sociological theorizing, was used systematically by Simmel in such classical essays as those on the role of the stranger, the role of the actor, or the role of the arbitrator.[32] Through Robert Park and other members of the Chicago school, the concept slowly filtered into American thought and was finally clearly and succinctly defined in the able work of Ralph Linton.[33]

These few introductory remarks can only suggest the variety, fruitfulness, and appeal of Simmel's work. No summary can possibly do full justice to it. There is just no substitute for reading Simmel. If this volume leads readers previously unacquainted with Simmel's thought to turn to his writings, it will have served its purpose.

[31] Coser, *op. cit.*

[32] On the role of the actor, see "Zur Philosophie des Schauspielers" in *Fragmente und Aufsätze, op. cit.* The other two types are discussed in *The Sociology of Georg Simmel, op. cit.*

[33] Ralph Linton, *The Study of Man* (New York: Appleton-Century-Crofts, Inc., 1936), Chap. 8.

# PART ONE

# SIMMEL'S STYLE OF WORK

PSYCHOLOGICAL EXPLANATIONS of the characteristics of scientific or artistic innovators abound in the literature. Sociological explanations are much less common. Such an explanation is offered in the following pages, where an effort is made to account for the peculiarities of Simmel's style of work in terms of his marginal role within the academy of the Germany of his time. His nonconformity and innovation are explained, at least in part, in terms of his academic role and the pressures exerted by the social structure of the academy. A revealing contemporary document is appended.

# THE STRANGER IN THE ACADEMY

## LEWIS A. COSER[1]

CONTEMPORARIES OF Georg Simmel often remarked upon peculiarities in his style of work—peculiarities that distinguished his work in a rather striking manner from that of other major sociologists. They stressed the dazzling brilliance of his writings and the brittle elegance, but they also noted the lack of sytematic exposition and the almost studied disorderliness of his method.

More recently, Kurt H. Wolff observed that "Simmel often appears as though in the midst of writing he were overwhelmed by an idea, by an avalanche of ideas, and as if he incorporated them without interrupting himself, digesting and assimilating only to the extent granted him by the onrush."[2]

Until now it has been generally assumed that these characteristics of Simmel's style might possibly be attributed to his personality and that sociological perspective was hence unlikely to provide significant clues for its understanding. I shall attempt in the following pages to show that this assumption may be unwarranted and that significant insights into what may first appear to be a purely psychological problem might be gained if we consider Simmel's role within the academic structure of the Germany of his

From *The American Journal of Sociology*, LXIII, 6 (May 1958), 635-41. (Originally entitled "Georg Simmel's Style of Work: A Contribution to the Sociology of the Sociologist.") Reprinted by permission of the publishers, The University of Chicago Press.

[1] This paper has greatly profited from a critical reading of an earlier version by Robert K. Merton of Columbia University, Kurt H. Wolff of Ohio State University, and Rose L. Coser of Wellesley College. I am grateful to them.

[2] Kurt H. Wolff (ed.), *The Sociology of Georg Simmel* (New York: The Free Press of Glencoe, Inc., 1950), p. xix.

time as well as his status in the intellectual community.[3] Sociological perspective may give us clues other perspectives fail to provide. Such an approach aims, to quote Robert K. Merton, to teach us something "about the processes through which social structures generate the circumstances in which infringement of social codes constitute a 'normal' (that is to say, an expectable) response." [4]

Simmel's biographers have remarked upon the fact that Simmel, though generally considered one of the leading intellects of his time, never received the academic recognition he seemed so amply to deserve.[5] For fifteen years Simmel lectured as a *Privatdozent* at Berlin University. Within the German university system of the time a position of *Privatdozent* indicated an apprenticeship status, that of an unpaid novitiate in the hope of making an academic career.[6] However, while still a *Privatdozent,* Simmel published a number of his most significant works.[7] It would seem, then, that Simmel, who had achieved wide renown as a philosopher and sociologist, still had not attained a status within the academy commensurate with his intellectual achievements and his scholarly productivity. While he was generally viewed as a mature scholar, he was structurally still in an apprentice status within the academy.

In 1900 Simmel was finally promoted to the rank of *Ausserordentlicher Professor.* The reader who may be unfamiliar with the structure of German universities before World War I should be reminded here that *Extraordinarii* were then not members of the faculty. They had no full standing within the academy and no decision-making power; they were shut off from participation in its affairs and were most insecure financially.[8] Theirs was an auxiliary and marginal status. Yet Simmel, by now a world-famous scholar,

---

[3] For earlier attempts at a sociology of the academy see several contributions to Max Scheler (ed.), *Versuche einer Soziologies des Wissens* (Munich: Dunker und Humblot, 1924), especially the papers by Max Scheler, Paul Honigsheim, and Helmuth Plessner.

[4] *Social Theory and Social Structure,* rev. ed. (New York: The Free Press of Glencoe, Inc., 1957), pp. 131-32.

[5] Cf. Nicholas J. Spykman, *The Social Theory of Georg Simmel* (Chicago: The University of Chicago Press, 1925), pp. xxiii-xxix; Wolff, *op. cit.,* pp. xxiii-xix.

[6] Cf. Abraham Flexner, *Universities* (New York: Oxford University Press, Inc., 1930), pp. 324 ff.

[7] See Erich Rosenthal and Kurt Oberlaender, "Books, Papers, and Essays by Georg Simmel," *American Journal of Sociology,* XL (November 1945), 238-47.

[8] Flexner, *op. cit.,* pp. 234 ff. and 354 ff.

occupied this position for practically the rest of his career. He was given a full professorship in the provincial University of Strasbourg in 1914, but he soon fell ill and died in 1918.

This is not the place to consider in detail the reasons why Simmel was assigned inferior status within the academy. Anti-Semitism, academic jealousy, the feeling among some of his colleagues that his was a "destructive" rather than a "constructive" intellect—all these seemed to have played a part.[9] Our concern here is less with the process through which status incumbents are selected and recruited than with the consequences that the incumbency of certain status positions is likely to have for the incumbent; our concern here is with role behavior rather than with role allocation.

It may be argued that Simmel's inferior status was itself a consequence of his particular style of work. But, even if it could be shown that Simmel's style of work in his earlier writings often called forth negative judgments from his professional status superiors, we must still ask why, instead of attempting to conform more closely to the expectations of the senior members of the academy, he persisted in publishing works that proved to be similar in style to his earlier contributions. Why did he disregard the negative sanctions of members of the academy and accentuate those characteristics that they could be expected to disapprove?

Expectations of colleagues and superiors within the faculty typically exert pressure upon the incumbent of junior-status positions to live up to the rules of the academic game. These rules require, among other things, intellectual discipline, the observance of fixed standards of scholarship, respect for the boundaries of the various specialized fields, attention to the contributions of senior men, and so on.[10] Those who attempt to create *ab ovo* are likely to be considered "unreliable," "outsiders," and hence to be mistrusted. As Plessner has argued: "Only those who are capable of developing the new out of the old fit into the framework of scholarship." [11] Any reader of Simmel will be well aware that his work hardly lived

[9] Marianne Weber, *Lebenserinnerungen* (Bremen: Johs. Storm, 1948), pp. 385-86; Wolff, *op. cit.*; Spykman, *op. cit.*
[10] See Helmuth Plessner, "Zur Soziologie der modernen Forschung," in *Versuche einer Soziologie des Wissens, op. cit.*, pp. 407-25; Logan Wilson, *The Academic Man* (New York: Oxford University Press, Inc., 1942).
[11] Plessner, *op cit.*, p. 422.

up to these norms. It should therefore not be too surprising that he encountered powerful opposition among representative academic role partners, apparently quite early in his career.

But if Simmel did not conform to these expectations, although surely desiring to be accepted in the academy, we are led to inquire whether the academic structure itself did not offer him opportunities for an alternative type of behavior. The concept of *role-set*, recently introduced by Robert K. Merton, may serve us well here: a social status, Merton argues, involves not a single associated role but an array of associated social roles. Merton calls attention to the fact that role partners who are differentially located in the social structure may have differing expectations as to the behavior of a person occupying a particular status.[12] So it seems to have been with the position of university instructor at Simmel's time. This position may entail, for those so inclined, a set of roles differing rather pronouncedly from the purely scholarly role. The German university teacher was expected to contribute to ongoing scholarship, and thus to address himself to his colleagues, but he was also expected to lecture to students. Many preferred to keep their lecture work at a minimum or to restrict it to work in small seminars with selected students. Others, among them Simmel, gave considerable emphasis to their activity as lecturers. Academic colleagues and superiors, however, were often rather ambivalent with respect to members of the faculty who spent what they considered excessive time in lecturing. What Logan Wilson has said about the American academy, where lecturing is a much more important and highly priced activity than in the German university, applies a fortiori to the latter:

> The chief acclaim of the teacher comes from below, which source is not important as a means of raising one's status. The acclaim from one's peers is frequently of the sort that decries too much attention to teaching, and belittles the popular teacher as a mere showman.[13]

While the popular teacher may incur the displeasure of peers, he may in exchange gain the approval of other role partners—his

[12] Merton, *op. cit.*, pp. 369 ff. Merton defines *role-set* as "that complement of role relationships which persons have by virtue of occupying a particular social status."

[13] Wilson, *op. cit.*, p. 192.

lecture public or audience.[14] But, in effect, he lives up to expectations distinct from those of his peers and superiors. This presents a major structural basis for the possible disturbance of a stable role-set among university teachers who have the ability to be popular. The audience does not necessarily judge the lecturer in terms of his systematic and methodical gathering of evidence and his disciplined pursuit of painstaking research endeavors but rather in terms of the brilliance of his performance, the novelty of his ideas, and the ability to fascinate.

All contemporary accounts agree that Simmel lived up to such expectations superlatively. He was considered one of the most brilliant, if not the most brilliant, lecturer of his time. He attracted students from the most varied disciplines; foreign visitors; unattached intellectuals from the world of publishing, journalism, and the arts; and a goodly number of members of "society" in search of intellectual stimulation. It is no exaggeration to say that many of Simmel's lectures were public events and often described as such in the newspapers.[15]

His style of delivery seems to have enthralled his audience. A contemporary writes:

> One could observe how the process of thought took possession of the whole man, how the haggard figure on the lecture platform became the medium of an intellectual process the passion of which was expressed not in words only, but also in gestures, movements, actions. When Simmel wanted to convey to the audience the core of an idea, he not only formulated it, he so to speak picked it up with his hands, his fingers opening and closing; his whole body turned and vibrated under the raised hand. . . . His intensity of speech indicated a supreme tension of thought; he talked abstractly, but this abstract thought sprang from lived concern, so that it came to life in the listener. . . .[16]

Another contemporary observer writes in a similar vein:

[14] Cf. Florian Znaniecki, *The Social Role of the Man of Knowledge* (New York: Columbia University Press, 1940).

[15] See, e.g., Emil Ludwig, "Simmel auf dem Katheder," *Die Schaubuehne*, X (April 1914), 411-13; Theodor Tagger, "Georg Simmel," *Die Zukunft*, LXXXIX (October 1914), 36-41; Paul Fechter, *Menschen und Zeiten* (Gütersloh: Berdelsmann, 1948), pp. 52-56.

[16] Fechter, *op. cit.*

He "thinks aloud" somebody said of him. One could add: He thinks visibly, one imagines seeing how a thought occurs to him. . . . One can see how his brain operates, how he joins ideas like a carpenter joins wood. . . . One is led to participate in the construction. One doesn't really listen, one participates in the thought process.[17]

Do we not have here some warranty to assume that, hurt and rebuffed as he may have been by the lack of recognition within the academy, Simmel came to rely increasingly on the approval of his lecture audience and hence to accentuate in his written style as well as in his oral delivery those characteristics that brought applause? It is interesting to note in this connection that, although his contemporaries have indicated that Simmel's audience gained the impression that he was "thinking aloud" while he lectured, so that they imagined that they—the listeners—were, so to speak, assisting, he was in actual fact wont to give some lectures several times with virtually no changes.[18] It would seem that Simmel cared so much for audience reaction that at times, like Churchill in a later day, he deliberately gave the impression before his audience that he was struggling with his ideas when he had, in fact, worked out his thoughts long before. This he may have done to enlist and maintain the interest of his audience.

Not only Simmel's lectures but the bulk of his writings also exhibited the characteristics that his lecture audiences prized. The unmatched brilliance of some of his essays is clearly related to the brilliance of his oral delivery; in fact, many of his essays, if not most, were first presented in lecture form.

In his published papers Simmel addressed himself much more frequently to the nonacademic audience. The bibliography compiled by Rosenthal and Oberlaender[19] reveals that, of the 180 articles published in his lifetime in various journals, newspapers, and reviews, only 64 were published in scholarly journals, while 116 appeared in nonscholarly publications destined for a wider cultivated public such as liberal newspapers, art magazines, and literary monthlies.[20]

[17] Tagger, *op. cit.*
[18] Fechter, *op. cit.*
[19] Rosenthal and Oberlaender, *op. cit.*
[20] Kurt Wolff's supplementary bibliography lists an additional twenty contributions to nonscholarly journals and only two to scholarly journals (*op. cit.*, pp. liv-lv).

This tells us about his reading public, but it does not give us sufficient evidence to support our claim that the academy's negative sanctions pushed Simmel to seek approval elsewhere. His non-academic orientation, after all, could be an index of his secondary interest in the academy.

We have claimed that Simmel's development was part of a social process in which he addressed himself to two publics—his scholarly colleagues, on the one hand, and his eager listeners, on the other. We have implied that his success with nonspecialized audiences met with further negative sanctions from his colleagues and induced him to seek success with a nonacademic audience. Such a claim can be supported only if we can follow Simmel's development over time. Since his published articles are on record, a simple count of their publications in various reviews and papers, distinguishing between dates of appearance, can be used as an index.

While Simmel was still a *Privatdozent,* his hopes of being accepted in the academy must have been higher than later, when recognition was not forthcoming. If we distinguish between the periodical writings published before the turn of the century (i.e., during the time he served as a *Privatdozent)* and later years, we find that in the earlier period 50 per cent of his writings appear in scholarly journals, as against only 28 per cent in the latter (See Table 1).[21]

### Table 1

#### Period of Publication of Simmel's Papers by Type of Journal

| Journal Type | Before 1900 No. | Before 1900 Per Cent | After 1900 No. | After 1900 Per Cent | Total No. |
|---|---|---|---|---|---|
| Scholarly | 31 | 50 | 33 | 28 | 64 |
| Nonscholarly | 31 | 50 | 85 | 72 | 116 |
| Total | 62 | 100 | 118 | 100 | 180 |

[21] It would be possible, we believe, to show that what holds true for Simmel's published papers in the periodical press also applies to his books. But this would involve a somewhat complex content analysis, which we cannot undertake at this time. Yet even a cursory glance at the bibliography will show that Simmel's more systematic and scholarly work was mainly published in the earlier stages of his career.

At the start of his career Simmel apparently communicated with both scholarly and nonscholarly audiences; later he tended to publish more and more in nonscholarly publications.[22] Earlier, he still attempted to live up to the expectations of the academy; in later years, while he was not unmindful of the academy, the nonacademic audience loomed larger.[23]

We have said enough to make it at least plausible that Simmel's self-image must have been molded to a large extent by the particular audience which rewarded him and that his intellectual production was influenced by the saliency of the demands that his non-academic role partners made on him. The pressures on his role set exerted by these role partners led to appropriate modifications of self-definitions and to appropriate role behavior. His auxiliary status in the academy exerted pressure on him to find a supportive audience at the margin of the academy, and the attempt to live up to their expectations which he had provoked involved him in a further process of alienation from the demands of the academy. As in the case of "The Stranger," of whom he wrote so perceptively and so movingly,[24] his relations to the academy were a compound of nearness and remoteness. He was inorganically appended to the academy, yet he was an organic member of the group. He could afford to maintain such a difficult marginal role because he found support and encouragement among his nonacademic listeners.[25]

Simmel, the marginal man, the stranger, presented his academic peers not with a methodical, painstakingly elaborated system but with a series of often disorderly insights, testifying to amazing

[22] Though we are in no position to prove this, there are many indications that the audience to which he communicated by the spoken word was composed of the same type of individuals, often perhaps the same physical individuals, whom he addressed in the many nonscholarly journals for which he wrote.

[23] It might be, of course, that, as Simmel became progressively better known and esteemed by other than the academic audience, publishers of lay periodicals increasingly prevailed upon him to publish with them. In short, it may have been a case not only of Simmel's initiative in searching out another audience but also of a greater interest by the agents of that audience in what he had to say. This could be construed as an interactive process between Simmel and the lay audience, with the publishers acting as intermediaries.

[24] Wolff, *op. cit.*, pp. 402-408.

[25] It is interesting to note that Simmel had no disciples in the academy, though he exerted some influence, whereas he had many followers among the literary intelligentsia.

powers of perception. Yet Simmel's very quest for originality stemmed in part from his self-image as a scholar. The academy does not, of course, prize purely routine work; it requires that its members contribute original results[26]—such results to be achieved, however, through academically approved means, within the academic rules of the game. Simmel conformed to the goals of the academy, but he rejected the norms governing the ways and means for their attainment.[27] We have shown that his innovation can be accounted for, at least in part, in terms of his academic role-set, that is, by the pressures exerted by the very social structure of the academy. That structure led him to engage in nonconforming behavior but at the same time to the development and cultivation of originality. May we not discover here that academic disciplines sometimes profit from what is judged to be nonconformist behavior in some of their practitioners?[28] Nonconformist behavior can have both manifest and latent functions. The discipline of sociology owes manifold leads to Simmel's travail—leads that may serve as points of departure for generations of patient and methodical investigators.

## A CONTEMPORARY ACADEMIC VIEW OF GEORG SIMMEL

The following letter was written in response to a request for an evaluation of Simmel from the Kulturministerium of Baden. Simmel was then (1908) being considered for one of the two chairs of philosophy at Heidelberg, for which he had been recommended by Gothein and Max Weber.

The letter, which appears in a memorial volume by Michael Landmann and Kurt Gassen (*Buch des Dankes an Georg Simmel* [Munich: Duncker und Humblot, 1958]), was translated by Herbert Menzel, of Columbia University. We are grateful to Arnold Simmel, of Columbia, for bringing the letter to our attention.

As you no doubt expect, I will express my opinion about Professor Simmel quite frankly. I do not know whether or not he has

[26] Cf. Robert K. Merton, "Priorities in Scientific Discovery," presidential address read at the Annual Meeting of the American Sociological Society, August 1957 (*American Sociological Review*, XXII [December 1957], 6).

[27] See Merton's "Social Structure and Anomie," in *Social Theory and Social Structure, op. cit.*, especially pp. 140-41.

[28] See, in this connection, Merton's crucial distinction between deviancy and nonconformity (*ibid.*, pp. 360-68).

been baptized, nor did I want to inquire about it. He is, at any rate, a dyed-in-the-wool Israelite, in his outward appearance, in his bearing, and in his manner of thinking. It is possible that this fact has stood in the way of his receiving a call abroad and of his promotion here (it is said that he was under consideration for a post in Vienna); but it is not necessary to adduce this fact by way of explanation. For his academic and literary merits and successes are very circumscribed and limited. His lectures are well attended. But it has long since been his habit to hold two-hour lectures, which are invariably in high demand in Berlin. He speaks exceedingly slowly, by dribs and drabs, and thus offers only little material, although it is well-rounded, succinct, and polished. These features are very much appreciated by certain categories of students who are very numerous here in Berlin. In addition, he spices his words with clever sayings. And the audience he recruits is composed accordingly. The ladies constitute a very large portion—even for Berlin. For the rest, there [appears at his lectures] an extraordinarily numerous contingent of the oriental world, drawing on those who have already settled here as well as on those who are still flooding in semester after semester from the countries to the East. His whole manner is in tune with their orientation and taste.

One does not come away from his lectures with too much of positive value; but it is pleasant to be offered up this and that titillating stimulation or volatile intellectual pleasure. To this must be added the fact that a Semitic lecturer—wholly, partially, or philo-Semitic, whatever he is—will find fertile soil, no matter what the circumstances, at a university where the corresponding part of the student body numbers several thousand, given the cohesion that prevails in these circles.

I do not imagine that the University of Heidelberg would be especially advanced by attracting that kind to its lecture halls. In fact, it is impossible for me to believe that the level of Heidelberg would be raised by allowing even broader space than it already occupies among the faculty to the world view and philosophy of life which Simmel represents, and which, after all, are only too obviously different from our German Christian-classical education. I believe that such admixture as may be desirable for healthy development has been attained. After all, there can be only limited justification for tendencies which undermine and negate more than they lay foundations and build up, during an era which is inclined to set all pillars asway—and that not always out of scholarly zeal, but also out of a thirst for notoriety.

Simmel owes his reputation chiefly to his "sociological" activity. Upon it was based the request to grant him the (honorary) title of professor [at Berlin, on an earlier occasion—*Trans.*]. But this request was primarily supported by Schmoller, who is always so ready to engage in innovations. It is my view, however, that sociology has yet to earn its position as a scholarly discipline [*Wissenschaft*]. It is, in my opinion, a most perilous error to put "society" in the place of state and church as the decisive [*maszgebend*, literally, *yardstick-providing*] organ of human coexistence. It would not seem right to me to give official standing to this orientation at this early date, especially not at a university which is as important to state and nation as Heidelberg is to Baden and Germany—least of all in the person of one who operates more by wit and pseudo-wit [*geistreiches und geistreichelndes Denken*] than by solid and systematic thinking.

Nor can I find that one comes away with much of permanent value from Simmel's writings (insofar as they have become familiar to me). It is hardly possible to treat of the mental life of the metropolis in a sparser and more biased way than he did in his lecture of that title at the Gehe Foundation in Dresden. I believe that there are more desirable and productive occupants for Heidelberg's second chair of philosophy than Simmel.

I regret that I must render an unfavorable judgment. . . .

[Signed] *Dietrich Schaefer*

# PART TWO

# SIMMEL'S WORK
## AS SEEN THROUGH THE EYES
## OF HIS CONTEMPORARIES

THERE IS NO better way to gauge the impact of a thinker on his times than by the reception accorded his work by his peers. This volume includes, therefore, a sampling of the appraisals of Simmel's work by his contemporaries.

Émile Durkheim (1858-1917) expressed a great deal of interest in Simmel's work. He was responsible for full critical accounts of Simmel's books in *L'Année Sociologique* and he arranged for a translation of one of Simmel's essays in its first issue. Nevertheless, as his essay makes clear, he remained basically opposed to Simmel's distinctive approach.

Ferdinand Tönnies (1855-1936), dean of modern German sociology, appears to have adopted a more sympathetic stance, although it is apparent that he was unable to accept Simmel's ahistorical approach and was somewhat appalled by Simmel's seeming "frivolity" of style.

Leopold von Wiese (1876-    ), whose later work was clearly written under the shadow of Simmel's influence, was one of the first to point to the fruitfulness of Simmel's formal method—as his article readily testifies.

Célestin Bouglé (1870-1939), who worked very closely with Durkheim without ever becoming an orthodox Durkheimian, contributed a markedly more friendly appraisal of Simmel's work than that which Durkheim had made.

Finally, the French philosopher Alfred Mamelet was the first, in

1914, to devote an entire book to the analysis of Simmel's work. The chapter on Simmel's sociology is here reprinted in its entirety. It testifies to its author's admiration for Simmel's approach, even though it may be somewhat flawed by his evident intention of extolling Simmel in order to flay Durkheim.

# ONE

# SOCIOLOGY AND
# ITS SCIENTIFIC FIELD

ÉMILE DURKHEIM

A SCIENCE WHICH has barely begun to exist has, and initially is
bound to have, only an uncertain and vague sense of the area of
reality that it is about to approach, and the extent and the limits
of that area. It can gain a clearer picture only to the degree that it
proceeds with its studies. And the heightened awareness of its subject matter that it acquires in this way is of the greatest importance;
for the path of the scientist is the more secure the more orderly it
becomes; and the more methodical it is, the more exact is the
account that he can render of the territory he is invading.

Sociology has reached the point at which it is opportune to make
every effort to bring about such progress. If some reactionary critics,
unwittingly under the influence of the prejudice which always mil-
itates against the formation of new sciences, reproach sociology for
not knowing the precise subject matter with which it intends to
deal, they can be told that such ignorance is inevitable in the first
stages of study and that our science came into being only yesterday.
It must not be forgotten, especially in view of the favorable reception that sociology is given now, that, properly speaking, Europe did
not have as many as ten sociologists fifteen years ago. To this must
be added that it is asking too much of a science that it define its
subject matter with excessive precision, for the part of reality that
it intends to study is never neatly separated from other parts. In

From Kurt H. Wolff (ed.), *Émile Durkheim, 1859-1917: A Collection of Essays,
with Translations and a Bibliography* (Columbus, Ohio: Ohio State University
Press, 1960), pp. 335-59. Copyright © 1959 by the Ohio State University Press.
Translated by Kurt H. Wolff. Reprinted by permission of the translator and
the publisher.

fact, in nature everything is so connected that there can be neither a complete break in continuity nor any too-exact boundaries between the various sciences. Nevertheless, it is urgent that we obtain, if we can, a clear idea of what constitutes the domain of sociology, where this domain is found, and what signs serve us in recognizing the complex of the phenomena with which we must deal—even if we neglect to fix boundaries, which are necessarily indeterminate anyway. This problem is all the more urgent for our science, because if we do not attend to it, its province may be extended to infinity: there is no phenomenon—from physiochemical ones to properly social facts—which does not take place in society. Hence we must accurately isolate social facts and must show what it is that forms their unity in order to avoid reducing sociology to nothing but a conventional label applied to an incoherent agglomeration of disparate disciplines.

Georg Simmel has made a notable, an almost violent, effort to trace the limits of the subject matter of sociology. The basis of his argument is the idea that, if sociology is to be, it must constitute a particular system of investigations that are perfectly distinct from those of the sciences which have long existed under the names of *political economy, history of civilization, statistics, demography,* and so on. The difference lies in the fact that these other sciences study what occurs in society, not society itself. The religious, moral, and legal phenomena which they treat occur within particular groups; but these groups must themselves be the object of a different inquiry, one which is independent of these others; and it is precisely this independent study that constitutes sociology. With the help of the very society which they form, men living in society achieve many kinds of different ends—some religious, others economic, still others aesthetic, and so on; the special sciences have as their subject matter the particular processes by which these ends are attained. But these processes are not in themselves social—at least, they have a social character only indirectly and only insofar as they develop in a collective environment. These sciences, therefore, are not properly sociological. In the complex usually called *society,* there exist two kinds of elements which must be clearly distinguished: there is the content, the diverse phenomena that occur among the associated individuals; and there is the container, the association itself, within which such phenomena may be observed. Association is the only truly sociological thing, and sociology is the science of association in the abstract.

> Sociology must not seek its problems in the material of social life, but in its form. . . . It is on this abstract consideration of the social forms that the entire right of sociology to exist is founded, just as geometry owes its existence to the possibility of abstracting pure forms from material things.

But by what means is this abstraction given concrete form? If every human association develops with particular ends in view, how can one isolate association in general from the varied ends which it serves, and ascertain its laws?

> By putting together associations devoted to the most diverse purposes and eliminating what they have in common . . . the differences, presented by the particular ends around which societies form, mutually cancel each other out, and the social form alone appears. A phenomenon—the formation of parties, for instance—may be observed in the world of art as well as in those of politics, industry, or religion; if we trace what occurs in all these milieus, irrespective of the diversity of ends and interests, it will be possible to determine the laws of this particular manner of grouping. The same method will allow us to study domination and subordination, the formation of hierarchies, the division of labor, competition, and so forth.[1]

It seems that in this fashion sociology is furnished with a clearly defined subject matter. We think, however, that in reality such a conception serves merely to keep it tied to metaphysical ideology when it actually shows an irresistible need to emancipate itself from this sphere. We do not contest the right of sociology to constitute itself by means of abstractions because there is no science that could be established otherwise. The abstractions must be methodically disciplined, however, and must separate the facts according to their natural distinctions; otherwise, they are bound to

---

[1] Georg Simmel, "The Persistence of Social Groups," translated by Allison W. Small, *American Journal of Sociology*, III (1898), 633.

degenerate into fantastic constructions and vain mythology. The old political economy also claimed the right to make abstractions, and, in principle, it cannot be denied this right; but the use it made of it was vitiated because the basis of every one of its deductions was an abstraction that it had no right to make; that is, the notion of a man who, in his action, was moved exclusively by his personal interest. This hypothesis cannot be determined at first sight from the beginning of the investigations; we are able to evaluate the impulsive force which personal interest can exercise on us only after repeated observations and methodical comparisons. Without them, there is no way of ascertaining whether there is in us something definite enough that it can be isolated from the other factors of our conduct and be considered apart from them. Who can say that between egoism and altruism there is the decisive separation which common sense unreflectively erects between them?

To justify the method advanced by Simmel, more is needed than to refer to the sciences that proceed by abstraction—namely, proof that the abstraction espoused is undertaken according to the principles with which every scientific abstraction must conform. By what right are the container and the content of society separated, and separated so radically? Only the container is claimed to be of a social nature; the content is not, or only indirectly so. Yet there is not a single proof to confirm such an assertion which, though far from being accepted as a self-evident axiom, may yet overwhelm a student.

To be sure, not all that happens in society is social; but this cannot be said of all that occurs *in* and *through* society. Consequently, in order to eliminate from sociology the various phenomena which constitute the web of social life, one has to demonstrate that they are not the work of the collectivity, but come from wholly different origins to place themselves within the general framework constituted by society. We do not know whether this demonstration has been attempted or whether the research that such a demonstration presupposes has been initiated. Yet it is immediately clear that the collective traditions and practices of religion, law, morality, and political economy cannot be facts less social than are the external forms of the collectivity; and if one deepens the study of these facts, one's first impression is confirmed: everywhere we find society at work elaborating them, and their effect on social organization is evident. They are society itself, living and working. What a strange idea it would be to imagine the group as a sort of empty form of trivial cast that can indifferently receive any kind of material whatever! The claim is that there are arrangements which are encountered everywhere, whatever the nature of the ends attained. But clearly, all these ends, despite their divergences, have characteristics in common. Why should only these common characteristics, and not the specific ones, have social value?

Such abstraction is not only unsystematic in that its effect is to separate things that are of the same nature, but the result of it, which is intended to be the subject matter of sociology, lacks all specificity whatever. Indeed, what are the meanings of the expression *social forms* and *forms of association in general?* If one wanted to speak only of the manner in which individuals are placed in contact with one another in association, of the dimensions of association, of its density—in a word, of its external and morphological aspect—the notion would be definite; but it would be too restricted to constitute, by itself alone, the subject matter of a science. For it would be equivalent to reducing sociology to the exclusive investigation of the substratum on which social life rests. As a matter of fact, however, our author attributes to the term *social forms* a much more extended significance. By it he understands not only the modes of grouping, the static condition of association, but also the most general forms of social relations. The term refers to the largest forms of relations of every kind that mesh in society and to the nature of the phenomena with which we are presented as being directly pertinent to sociology—the division of labor, competition, imitation, or the state of the individual's liberty or dependence vis-à-vis the group. Between these relations and the other, more special ones, however, there is only a difference of degree. How can a simple difference of this sort justify so definite a separation between two orders of phenomena? If the former constitute the subject matter of sociology, why must the latter, which are of the same kind, be excluded from it? The basis which the proposed abstraction seems to constitute when the two are opposed as container and content dis-

appears once the significance of those words is more exactly specified, and it becomes clear that they are no more than metaphors,
inexactly applied.

The most general aspect of social life is not, for that matter, either
content or form, any more than it is any one of the special aspects
which social life shows us. There are not two kinds of reality which,
though intimately connected, are distinct and separable; what we
have instead are facts of the same nature, examined at different
levels of generality. And what, incidentally, is the degree of generality that such facts need in order to be classified among sociological phenomena? We are not told; and the question is one to
which there is no answer. This suggests how arbitrary such a criterion is and how it gives us free rein for extending the boundaries
of the science. While pretending that it defines research, it actually
leaves it to the fancy of the individual. There is no rule for deciding
in an impersonal manner where the circle of sociological facts begins and where it ends; not only are the boundaries mobile, which
is quite legitimate, but it is not clear why they should be located
at this point rather than at another. It must be added that, in order
to study the most general types of social actions and their laws, one
has to know the laws of more special types, since the former cannot
be investigated and explained without systematic comparison with
the latter. In this respect, every sociological problem presupposes a
profound knowledge of all those special sciences that should be
placed outside sociology but which sociology cannot do without.
And since such universal competence is impossible, one has to be
satisfied with summary knowledge, which is rapidly gathered and
cannot be subjected to any control.

These are the characteristics of Simmel's investigations. We appreciate their subtlety and ingenuity, but we think it impossible
to trace the main divisions of our science as he understands it in an
objective manner. No connection can be discovered among the
questions to which he draws the attention of sociologists; they are
topics of meditation that have no relation to an integral scientific
system. In addition, Simmel's proofs generally consist only of explanations by example; some facts, borrowed from the most disparate fields, are cited but they are not preceded by critical analysis,
and they often offer us no idea of how to assess their value. For

sociology to merit the name of a science, it must be something quite different from philosophical variations on certain aspects of social life, chosen more or less at random according to the leanings of a single individual. What is needed is the formulation of the problem in a way that permits us to draw a logical solution. . . .

# TWO

# SIMMEL AS SOCIOLOGIST

### FERDINAND TÖNNIES

AFTER SCHÄFFLE'S PRECEDENT, and apart from books of momentary importance, Simmel was the first to give the title *Soziologie (Sociology)* to a major work in the German language. The objection has been raised that the title does not correspond to the content, which offers nothing of a systematic nature. But Simmel appears to defend himself against this criticism in advance, by prefacing the work only with the demand that the reader keep firmly in mind throughout the book the question raised about the problem of sociology in the first chapter, "since otherwise these pages might appear as a collection of unrelated facts and reflections." Thus to characterize this insightful work would, however, be an injustice, for the subtitle, *Investigations into the Forms of Association (Vergesellschaftung)*, sufficiently indicates that Simmel was concerned only with theory. . . .

*On Social Differentiation: Sociological and Psychological Investigations* (1890), the work which first established Simmel's name, contains his fundamental methodological ideas, so that its fifth chapter, "On the Intersection of Social Circles," is partly taken over into the larger work. At the time, I said in a discussion of the little volume that there remained in it something at times unsure and perhaps even unfinished. I would not dare to make this criticism of the later sociological works; rather, it seems as if this unfinished quality had here become a special art, characterized by suggestion, shading, halftones, and seemingly magical light effects. It is more than a coincidence that Simmel, who in his last years wanted to be entirely

From *Frankfurter Zeitung* (October 9, 1918), translated by Martin Nicolaus. Reprinted by permission of the publishers.

a philosopher and had a special love for aesthetics, selected Rembrandt as his hero.

The title of that earliest work is significant in another way: differentiation is the very mark of Simmel's thought. It contains much of the wisdom of that old style of thinking which has been described as a mental facility for inventing unexpected similarities. His mind, it has been said, is totally set upon analysis; and this, of course, is correct. Social objects are for him always given conditions (*Gegebenheiten*) whose essence he seeks to discover by approaching them, so to speak, with the psychological knife, differentiating them and illuminating them by revealing their elements. It has been said that, in this process, he sometimes grinds them to a fine dust so that, in the end, nothing remains but a homeopathic dilution to which only faith can give an immanent essentiality. In reality, however, Simmel did not lack synthetic capability (although he rarely used it) so much as he lacked that vision and intuitive power which can grasp the uniqueness (*das Eigentümliche*) of elemental forces and motives and show the meaning of that uniqueness within the larger context of all life.

His investigations, therefore, rarely concern themselves with large-scale historic phenomena of social life. No matter how many remarkable examples his profound erudition marshals in support of his fine differentiations, he prefers to seize upon completely timeless, general problems, such as super[ordination] and subordination, conflict, secret societies, self-preservation of the social group, the spatial ordering of society, the expansion of the group, and the development of individuality. These are all significant objects, and he treats them with a multiplicity of charming observations, brilliant insights, and blinding dialectics; but he never fully attains the recognition that the most proper objects of sociological inquiry are the social structures (*Gebilde*) which arise out of the thoughts of men themselves, out of their subjects. To distinguish sharply all mental objects (*Gedankendinge*), such as alliances and leagues, clubs and cooperative societies, parishes and states, churches and orders, from the "groups" and "circles" which are externally recognizable—that, in my opinion, is the precondition for the solution of the specifically sociological problem. It must be said that Simmel stubbornly avoided seeing this fact. His real achievements must therefore be relegated more to social psychology—a field which, admittedly, was little enough cultivated—rather than to sociology proper. But in that field lay his real excellence. One can best grasp the magical versatility of his highly skillful thought by looking through the index of the volume which he entitles *Soziologie*. But the most important thing, from the scientific point of view, will be found wherever he most closely approaches the proper object of sociology, as for example in the fifth chapter, on secrecy and secret societies, and in the eighth, on the self-preservation of the group. And in a different direction we find the same thing in the *Philosophy of Money* which has justly received so much attention. Here he is dealing with an objective structure (*Gebilde*) which confronts the subjective mind "as norm." Simmel well knows that this has a far wider relevance, but he does not develop its importance further.

Thus even the most recent little book, *Fundamental Questions of Sociology*, clings to the notion that the most general form of "association" is reciprocity (*Wechselwirkung*), and charmingly elaborates that the latter's "play-form" is conviviality (*Geselligkeit*), which, he says, is related to its concrete form as the work of art is to reality! One remembers that on the night before the opening of the first Congress of Sociologists in Frankfurt (1910) Simmel presented his delicate meditations about the sense of liberation and relief which precisely the more profound men find in conviviality. If these observations approach coquetry, if elsewhere—in a "sociology of the senses"—Simmel makes perfume accomplish "a unique synthesis of individual-egotist and social teleology in the olfactory sense," nevertheless all such spiritual amusements were meant in earnest and in the most profound sense. Yet they were not suited for advancing recognition of the enormous complexities of social life and, to some extent, even provoked a ridicule they did not deserve.

The meritorious achievement of Simmel is not confined to sociology alone. But here also this insightful man will leave profound traces. German scholarship has lost in him one of its brightest lights. He, too, fell in the turmoil of World War [I], as Lamprecht, Lexis, Schmoller, and Wagner had before him. None of them saw its outcome, and all were spared the anxiety which we must bear about the future of the German spirit and the future of European humanity.

# THREE

# SIMMEL'S FORMAL METHOD

## LEOPOLD VON WIESE

GEORG SIMMEL's *Sociology* is today understandably viewed with the greatest interest by all those who believe in the future of sociology as a science. Although these *Investigations into the Forms of Association* are broad in scope, the work is fragmentary and incomplete, as its author intended it to be. He would not—could not—present a complete, closed system; the only aim of the book is to clarify his fundamental conception of the problem of sociology by means of a series of applications. The author states:

> As a consequence [of the basic conception], it is out of the question to attempt anything more than to begin and to point out the direction of an infinitely long path; and any systematically final completeness would be, at the least, self-deception. An individual can attain completeness here only in the subjective sense, by reporting everything he has succeeded in observing.[1]

This is a very important advance over the older sociologists, who foundered on their mania for systems (I need mention only Ratzenhofer). To this rejection of completeness, Simmel adds the narrow delimitation of sociology as a science. It is to his credit that he has clarified the difference between the general modern tendency to view the objects of various sciences sociologically (but without detracting from their independence and autonomy), and the creation of sociology as a new science. Because of the intellectual demands of the present age, it is more and more frequently recognized today

From Leopold von Wiese, "Neuere soziologische Literatur," in *Archiv für Sozialwissenschaft und Sozialpolitik*, XXXI (1910), 897-901. Translated by Martin Nicolaus. Reprinted by permission of the author.

[1] Georg Simmel, *Soziologie* (Leipzig: Duncker und Humblot, 1908), p. 17.

that the objects of the traditional humanities (cultural and moral sciences [*Geisteswissenschaften*]) find realization only within the framework of society. This sociological *method* in the moral sciences is the legacy of the nineteenth century. The establishment of sociology is an altogether different thing. Although the latter cannot bring new facts, new material, to light, it draws "a new line through otherwise well-known facts." [2] It establishes new points of view, new abstractions. The various older social sciences have as their objects the contents of social processes, corresponding to the particular real areas of social life (such as economics, jurisprudence, and so on); sociology, however, examines the *forms* of association. That is to say, it examines the phenomena of human cooperation, altruistic and antagonistic interaction, the modes of reciprocal influence and mutual interpenetration in all their numberless purposes and diverse contents. The manifold forms in which association is realized are to be conceptually released from these diverse contents and analyzed as psychic phenomena of a special kind. But despite this [socio]psychological basis, sociology is in no sense a branch of psychology. Although sociology deals predominantly with psychic facts, it does not do so in order to discover the laws of psychic processes; the aim of sociology is, rather, to grasp the "objectivity of association" (which, however, as was said, is "carried by psychic processes"). In the same way that, on the one hand, psychology and sociology are not identical, so, on the other hand (and as in all special sciences), social science proper is distinct from its epistemology and its metaphysics. According to Simmel, the question of the position of society in the cosmos belongs to the metaphysics of sociology, while sociological epistemology includes the questions "Is society possible?" and "Does society exist outside of us or only in our consciousness?" and the like; so that these problems are relegated, like their metaphysical counterparts in philosophy, to defined subdisciplines.

Here Simmel has eliminated all of sociology's claims to encyclopedic-universal significance, all pretension that it ought to be the all-inclusive integration of the particular social sciences. Nor is he the least interested in extending the perspective of the natural sciences to the facts of human society. But, as indicated, Simmel

[2] *Ibid.*, p. 4.

limits the task of sociology even further: the content-material of social relations is to play as small a role as possible in this social science; he is interested only in the formal aspects of association. A question arises: Is such a limitation to the forms of association possible? The chapters of his work are well worth reading (their specific content cannot be examined here); but does the way in which Simmel carries out his program demonstrate the possibility and the fruitfulness of his method?

To begin with, one must beware of considering form as incidental or subordinate to content. The essence of a thing is often more clearly revealed in its form than in its content. And so it is in this case: by ignoring the content of social interrelations as much as possible, one may achieve a liberation from coincidental, temporary, unessential elements—and this alone makes possible a more profound insight into human nature as such. Hitherto-veiled secrets of the human mind, potential for human development, human motives and aspirations only now become clear. The essence of culture is not revealed by searching for it in too much concreteness—in compact, hard particularities and their summations. This external narrowing of the field of sociology signifies a valuable deepening, an internal expansion of its power of insight.

In posing the problem of sociology, I can never let the one goal out of sight: the image of man and of society must be purified of prejudice; it must emerge from our scrutiny more clearly and more genuinely than has hitherto been possible, without sociology, through metaphysical ethics and traditional political and cultural philosophy. In my opinion, Simmel's method brings us nearer to this goal (no matter to what extent Simmel may be motivated by purely abtract, scientific aims; no matter how much he may perhaps consider his social forms as ends in themselves). To that extent I am ready to consider his way as correct, and to see in his sociology a significant advance over all past attempts. But it seems to me that this science of the forms of association is in need of certain guiding ideas—of a unified goal—if it is to proceed from repeated analyses to the attainment of a concluding synthesis. This is especially true of Simmel's work: as far as I can tell, his investigations run the danger of ending in scattered fragments. Surely they contain not only a great many fine observations, but also peaks of the most

valuable insight; but they lose themselves in playing with the
fullness of forms with the subtlest and nicest of nuances. At times
the interweaving of his thoughts resembles a spider's web studded
with glittering drops of dew; but a substantial breeze can destroy
it. The danger of his thread of thought becoming unravelled would
have been avoided had Simmel established solid fundamental conceptions to carry the system. Above, I made no objection to Simmel's fragmentalism; in *Sociology* this is understandable and proper.
But it is another question whether or not Simmel is at all capable
of overcoming this tendency. I entertain doubts as to whether his
analytic method can ever reach synthesis. This does not diminish
his scientific importance. But when one is forced to pass judgment
on the direction in which he wants to lead sociology, then one must
indeed ask whether this fragmentary and incomplete character is
not a disadvantage intimately linked with the essence of his thought.
Unless I am greatly mistaken, Simmel has already published on
various other occasions, as independent essays, many of the individual chapters dealing with the problem he poses.[3] I must say
that they impressed me as more effective when they were thus separated. Here, where they are side by side as parts of a whole, the lack
of transition from one to another is striking. Out of the numerous
notions about the manifold forms of association there does not
emerge a central doctrine of the forms of association. The distinction between the form of association and its content is much more
comprehensible in any single essay than it is here, where the formal
analyses are compiled in a great heap, without any systematic sus-
taining connection. In any case, this accumulation of thought-frag-
ments is readable as a sequence only because of the fact that, with
all his tendency toward abstraction, Simmel is by no means clumsy
in dealing with concepts (*kein "Begriffskrüppel"*); that is, his presentation has great aesthetic attractiveness. From a certain aspect I
would even call his sociology the sociology of an aesthete, a sociology
for the literary salon. Simmel is a cultural psychologist with a cos-
mopolitan cast of mind. In his work we never encounter mere
book-wisdom or dry, pedantic erudition; rather, one feels the rich
internal agitation of the explorer: his examples are vivid, interesting, psychologically well-selected, and presented with individual

[3] *Ibid.*, Chaps. 2-10.

originality. In short, inner experience means more to him than dry scholarship. But in its mosaic form and its aestheticism, this sociology has a distinctly personal, Simmelean character. The same method in the hands of Mr. ———— (no, I had better name no names!) would be unbearable. And so I would reach the following summary:

The limitation of sociology to the doctrine of the forms of association seems to me an important advance capable of introducing clarity into a great deal of confusion. But even more important than this establishment of an independent discipline is the transition to the sociological *method* in the existing particular branches of cultural science. To elaborate the sociological aspects of economics, jurisprudence, ethics, religion, philology, geography, and so on—*that* is of primary importance.

# FOUR

# THE SOCIOLOGY OF GEORG SIMMEL

## CÉLESTIN BOUGLÉ

IN THE LARGE volume which he entitles *Sociology: Investigations into the Forms of Association,* Simmel claims that he is not offering a system but rather a great number of examples designed to show the kinds of generalizations one can make in sociology; and he does this if only that he might be able to use what Descartes described as the appropriate "bias."

Why is it that history neither is nor can be a science? Perhaps it is because, in the last analysis, the subject matter of history is a fluid complexity which must be grasped in its totality. And so it is not surprising either that the study of history should reveal more variations than consistencies, or that historians should find it difficult to establish causality between the myriad of occurrences. However, if one agreed to limit himself to a particular perspective and to abstract from the variations in content so as to focus only on the constant forms, then he would, perhaps, arrive at a series of observations the significance of which would extend beyond the range of the particular fact. It was by abstraction—i.e., by concerning itself only with spatial forms—that geometry established itself; and it was by abstraction that linguistics established itself as the science concerned with linguistic forms. Similarly, one could establish sociology as the discipline concerned only with social forms.

Of course, in one sense everything is social—just as, in one sense, everything is psychological; but we have been able to progress in our understanding of the functions of the mind without taking into

From *La Philosophie Allemande au XIX^me Siècle* (Paris: Félix Alcan, 1912). Translated by Jon Gower Davies. Reprinted by permission of Presses Universitaires de France.

account the various subject matters with which these functions are concerned. In the same way it is possible to study the modes and effects of sociation without being concerned with the various ends which sociation serves. In a word, it is possible to study what happens *in* society by looking at what happens *because of* society. The proof of this lies in the fact that the forms of sociation vary independently of social ends and social ends vary independently of the forms of sociation. Undoubtedly content influences form, but it does not determine it. Whatever the *ends* of an association—whether political, religious, or economic—it is legitimate to examine it to see how parties are organized, how work is divided, and how competition is organized among its members. It is Simmel's concern to emphasize those phenomena which are common to the workings of diverse associations. Whatever the substantive nature of the societies he might examine, he will subject them to an abstract analysis aimed at discovering how, for example, the relations among individuals vary according to whether superiority is vested in one individual, conceded to a group, or incarnated in some principle above and beyond the group as well as to the individual. Again, when he talks of competition, it is not in order to study a specific example of competition—whether economic, religious, or aesthetic—but to study the functions of conflict in general, so as to see what kinds of alliances it involves, by what means the social order defends itself against the divisive consequences to which conflict might give rise, and so on. The same approach determines his interest in secret societies, whether these are groups of conspirators or of thieves, of visionaries or of debauchees. His approach would lead him to try to discover the typical interrelations which secret societies, precisely because they are secret, tend to institute among their members.

From all this we can see that, when Simmel talks of social forms, he doesn't simply mean the external forms of society. *L'Année Sociologique* groups under the title *social morphology* everything that concerns land and population—i.e., the geographical and demographical bases of the existence of collectivities. As far as Simmel is concerned, the study of these two topics constitutes but a small part of social morphology. Although he certainly pays attention to a completely "external" fact (such as the social significance of numbers and their variations), he also utilizes information about an institution (such as an aristocratic regime), about a process (such as competition), and about a quality (such as the secret character of a group).

It is difficult to summarize the intricacies of Simmel's extremely ingenious and subtle insights, and perhaps it would be best to indicate the results he gets from his approach by offering a few illustrative examples.

When discussing superiority, we said that it can be exercised by an individual, by a group, or by a collective principle which stands over and above individuals. We must trace the consequences of these various hypotheses.

A group of individuals may be subordinated to an individual who either represents or opposes them, but usually in either case the subordination has the effect of unifying the group. This fact explains the principal advantage of monarchies: they establish unity among the population. It might well be that the Greek city-states decayed because they lacked a superior authority which, by dominating the several parties, could have unified them. Furthermore, this unity can take one of two forms: it can be either leveling or hierarchical. Sometimes the dominating person endeavors to impose universal degradation on all his subjects; from this is derived the well-known relationship between despotism and egalitarianism. At other times the dominating person may cede some fraction of power to—or find himself deprived of some fraction of power by—one or more of the diverse and numerically unequal strata of society. Thus the latter, in turn, come to possess varying degrees of influence over the uses of power. In both cases, the supremacy of the ruler is explained by the fact that, although the subjects subordinate but a segment of their personalities, the ruler dominates them by mobilizing the full force of his personality. Supremacy and personality are intimately linked.

The character of the relationship between superior and subordinate is noticeably different when domination is exercised by a group of persons rather than by a single individual. The subjects may find themselves either more harshly or more justly treated. Domination by a group is impersonal and, because of this, it is less arbitrary; but it also means that less consideration is given to the personalities

of the subordinates. Domination may be exercised through the inter-
mediation of agents (though this is a very specific sociological phenomenon, occurring only in societies which are already developed).
When it is, it assumes a quite special quality. When exercised ad-
ministratively, domination may be more severe in one case and less
severe in another.

Superordination may at times belong, not to one group, but to
two; in this case the subordinates find it easier to reduce the extent
of their dependency. Yet, again, if they are totally without initiative
they tend to suffer more because of the plurality of their rulers: "It
is not good to have two masters." If they [the subordinates] retain
even a minimum of liberty, they would do well to exploit the divisions among their superiors: *duobus litigentibus tertius gaudet.*
During the *ancien régime* the Third Estate was *tertius gaudens*
between the monarchy and the feudal nobility. Moreover, groups
which are superior to another group are seldom completely equal
among themselves; there are degrees of supersubordination among
them, and this results in that essentially sociological phenomenon:
hierarchy. As hierarchical gradations become rationalized, they lessen the intensity of the subordination, because the subordinate is
now provided with a means of recourse against his immediate superior.

The supremacy of a principle, of an impersonal idea elevated
over and above individuals, also serves to render subordination less
onerous to the subordinated. It has the effect of bringing even the
superiors into the ranks of the subordinates: they become obliged to
render allegiance to the very order which they themselves first
promulgated and prestige, in some way, gets detatched from them
and becomes attached to the principle they represent or to the function they fulfill. Under the sway of a principle, superiority is legiti-
mized by its coincidence with the common interest; thus, the
inferior has the feeling of working alongside his superior. The relationship of subordination undergoes a change, subjectively speaking, and becomes one of cooperation.

There are two main ways in which society might develop so that
individuals could regard themselves as equals. It might develop in
such a way that the various positions of power could be, and in fact

are, filled by different people; or it might develop into a series of
social circles which would enable the same individual to envisage
himself as superior in one aspect and inferior in another.

This does not mean that the relationship of subordination would
—or even could—disappear: it is essential to the continuance of
society. Yet, when superiority becomes detached from the personality of the individual to whom it was originally linked, then one can
hope that the state of subordination will continue to lose more and
more of the humiliating connotations it has for the subordinates.

One can expect that suggestive insights might be forthcoming
from an application of this method to the study of secret societies.
Simmel shows that, whether the group is of conspirators or of
thieves, of visionaries or of debauchees, the secret [society] has the
function of protection. If such societies are to fulfill their functions,
it is necessary for the members to have full confidence in one another. It is thus important that they should learn to keep silent
(and "the apprenticeship of silence" well may have been the best
training for moral intensity). It is also important that one word
of command should be able to get them to obey without question
and even without understanding. Because of this, formulas and
ritual practices are designed which are aimed at minimizing the
independence of the individual wills and maximizing their integration. And because of this comes the establishment of a strict
hierarchy in which the separate functions correspond to the various
stages of initiation. And so, precisely because they are secret, these
voluntary and highly self-conscious associations establish a rather
mechanical organization.

These summaries are too brief, and they lose the wealth of detail
which is so charming a facet of Simmel's analyses. Yet, they at least
enable us to catch a glimpse of the richness of the psychological
deductions with which his work abounds. Can this kind of sociology
be anything other than psychology? If one *were* to draw this conclusion, Simmel would not object. He confesses—or, rather, he
insists—that the interactions which seem to him to be the constitu-
ent elements of social life are, in fact, psychological phenomena.
And for him, as for Tarde, the analysis of mental interaction is the
essence of sociology. (We show elsewhere how extensive are the
similarities between Simmel's methods and of those of Tarde.)

Instead of studying the large-scale institutions (churches, political organizations, commercial enterprises) which dominate individuals and which, it seems, come to possess a life of their own, Simmel prefers to examine topics which to him are more fruitful; and so he studies sociation "at the moment of birth," or the relations and mutual influences among individuals. These serve to explain the lives of social entities just as intercellular physiochemical relations explain the life of the organism.

After all is said and done, social wholes have for Simmel but a provisional reality, and this must give way as we come to a better understanding of the interactions from which they are derived. For his part, he readily admits that a perfect science would ascribe reality only to individuals and their interactions; and he is satisfied only when he has directed our attention to a form of explanation based on elements, molecules, or the "social atoms."

Whichever way you look at it, Simmel's thought moves away from that of Durkheim and approaches that of Tarde.

It is all too easy to tell where these methods lead and to what conceptions they commit us. For Simmel, sociological explanations are descriptions of inner experiences—i.e., they are explanations which recount what happens in those small spheres called *souls* when these are brought into contact with one another. By their very nature, such explanations offer much in the way of speculation and little in the way of proof. Because of this, one often feels that Simmel's analyses, although extremely subtle, belong mostly to the realm of probability. His method has drawn severe criticism from those—both in the social sciences and in the other sciences—who are concerned with accumulating the greatest possible number of objective and methodically established truths. Sometimes his critics have shown themselves to be hostile toward a sociology of this type, which seems to stand midway between art and science. One can legitimately reply to this by stating that there is also room for this type of sociology. Even though Simmel's formulations may not go beyond the realm of probability, they are profound and intricate, and they should definitely be codified, classified, and offered for examination. And it is beyond doubt that, had Simmel chosen to be a more objective sociologist, he would have found it much more difficult to be so suggestive a "moralist."

# FIVE

# SOCIOLOGICAL RELATIVISM

## ALFRED MAMELET

SIMMEL'S CONCEPTION OF sociology is, from the outset, clearly opposed to contemporary French sociology. The latter is predicated upon regarding social facts as something possessing two characteristics: exteriority and constraint. French sociology has its origin in traditionalism and positivism. It is anti-individualist; and political and historical contingency has effected a link between this anti-individualism and the notion of the existence of a social order. Preoccupied above all with putting restrictions on individual initiative in areas of social and political organization, the traditionalists and Auguste Comte endeavored to show that the social order, like the physical order, has its own laws which are superior to individual wills, and that individuals cannot transgress these laws without precipitating grave calamity. Their concern for social organization and stability (a concern which would legitimize the state of French society as it was at the beginning and middle of the nineteenth century), and their concern to contain the revolutionary spirit supplies the explanation of the opposition which Comte and the traditionalists established between the individual and society. By working with this opposition as a base—i.e., by defining the social fact in terms of exteriority and constraint, and as standing over and against individual will—contemporary French sociology has persisted in excluding individual actions and interactions from the realm of sociological research. In fact, it has even tended to disregard them;

From A. Mamelet, *Le Relativisme philosophique chez Georg Simmel* (Paris: Librairie Félix Alcan, 1914), Chap. 6: "Le Relativisme sociologique," pp. 144-55. Translated by Jon Gower Davies. Reprinted by permission of Presses Universitaires de France.

and, consequently, it has neglected to study those forms of sociation which emphasize not the constraint of an institution, but the interaction of free individuals—i.e., all the forms of modern society. The Simmelian conception of sociology has the advantage over the Durkheimian conception in that it is much wider in scope and is thus applicable to liberal and democratic societies (in which the individual is a free agent, a voter or legislator, and as such an active force for progress) as well as to authoritarian societies (in which the mass and tradition are everything and the individual nothing). This does not mean that this emphasis leads Simmel to adopt the thesis held in France by Tarde. According to this thesis sociological facts are essentially psychological facts. Simmel is as concerned as Durkheim to establish sociology as an independent science, distinct both from psychology and history. But he tries to gain this status for sociology by utilizing concepts which are less abstract, less all-encompassing, and closer to concrete and living reality than the concepts of exteriority and constraint. These concepts—all of which can be grouped under a category which carries the full import of relativism, i.e., *reciprocity in interaction*—are, as we have seen, those of domination and subordination, of competition, of imitation, of opposition, of the division of labor, and so on. These are concepts which, while procuring the establishment of a specifically *sociological* (as opposed to a psychological or historical) form of explanation, can still leave room for all the varieties of individual action, from the most dependent to the most free. The relativist point of view has been able to provide a single answer to the problem which, in France, has resulted in the two separate answers of Durkheim and Tarde: namely, the problem of freeing sociology, as a science, from the tutelage of psychology while at the same time keeping it as close as possible to concrete reality.

This fundamental difference between Durkheim's conception of sociology and the Simmelian conception immediately gives rise to another important difference. According to Simmel, sociology should not limit itself, as does Durkheim's sociology, to the study of social macrocosms which are objectified, large-scale, synthetic, secondary, and detached from the human interactions from which they derive; it should show us the microcosmic structures of society and help us to grasp the detail of the processes of which large-scale institu-

tions—such as states, churches, corporations, the family and so on—
are the result. A comparison between the living organism and society might elucidate what is omitted by studying only macrocosms.
The large-scale institutions are to society what organs are to the
organism. Yet we understand the organs of the living body only
when we know how they are formed, and their formation is the
result of an infinity of intra[cellular] and intercellular processes.
Consequently, we must analyze these processes. The same is true for
society. The large-scale institutions which constitute the organs of
the social body cannot be properly understood unless one analyzes
the elementary processes from which they derive and which govern
the formation of the social tie. At the same time, it is necessary to
beware of drawing any false conclusions from this analogy between
the organism and society, for to Simmel it has a purely methodological significance:

> There is definitely no question here of any analogy, sociological or meta-
> physical, between social reality and organic reality. It is solely a ques-
> tion of an analogy in the *method* of studying those two orders of
> reality. It is a question of discovering the threads which have been spun,
> and the delicate relationships which have been established between men.
> The continual weaving of these relationships constitutes the basis of all
> those large-scale structures which attain objectification and aquire a life
> of their own. These altogether *primary* processes (which turn individual
> reality into social reality) are as deserving of formal analysis as are the
> events in, and formation of superior and complex structures [*sind
> also . . . der formalen Betrachtung zu unterziehen*]; and the reciproc-
> ities of particular actions which occur at this level and which hitherto
> have been unsubjected to theoretical examination must be envisaged
> as playing a part in the general process of sociation.[1]

Although these processes are, in point of fact, psychological processes, sociology can claim the right to analyze them because, as is
shown in *Probleme der Geschichtsphilosophie,* a distinction can
be made between—on the one hand—phenomena in the processes
which clearly obey the laws of psychology, and—on the other hand
—the function of these processes, which is amenable to analysis by
the forms of sciences other than psychology, in particular by the

[1] Georg Simmel, *Soziologie* (Leipzig: Duncker und Humblot, 1908), pp. 20-21.

forms of sociology: "The scientific study of psychic reality is not necessarily psychology." [2] This reality can be approached from different standpoints and can be grasped by different sciences.

It is of course a fact that when, for example, men influence each other, or when one man submits to something done by another, that this is a psychic phenomenon. Each particular instance of such a phenomenon can be comprehended only by the use of psychological methodology— i.e., by the use of hypotheses based on psychological constructs and by an interpretation of data which is rendered objective through the use of psychological categories. Yet the adoption of another scientific perspective enables one to by-pass the psychological analysis as such, and to go on to analyze, to examine, and to rearrange the content in such a way that it can be comprehended as coming under the concept of sociation.[3]

From this perspective—which is that of sociology as Simmel understands it—it is the forms of interpersonal relationships which restructure the subject matter: and these forms are precisely those which have already been listed—viz., domination, subordination, competition, imitation, opposition, and so on. . . .

Simmel feels that sociology gains the status of an independent science when and if it concerns itself with the study of these diverse forms of sociation. In *Soziologie* the study of these forms has already been carried out to a large extent and, although it is not necessary to go into the book in detail, it is necessary to trace its main outlines and to point out the major areas of interest. It is by utilizing the concept of *form* that, for example, Simmel tries to demonstrate the influence exercised on the internal structure of social groups by the size of the group. Then again, he seeks to determine the forms and the psychological conditions and the social consequences of domination, subordination, competition, and the struggle for life; or to unravel the effect of the necessity for secrecy on the structure of secret societies; or to examine the main forms and consequences of the encounter and intermeshing of social circles such as families, professions, nations, and so on. He tries to analyze the influence of poverty and wealth on social organization and on interpersonal relations. He tries to establish the conditions necessary for the

[2] *Ibid.,* p. 21.
[3] *Ibid.,* pp. 22-23.

conservation and perpetuation of groups (conditions which he finds in the incessant interaction between group members), and to determine the influence of space on social organization. Finally he seeks to understand the principal factors leading to the growth of societies and to the appearance of free and differentiated individuals. Although the book ends only after numerous digressions (one of the most intriguing being the analysis of the sociological significance of the senses, in particular [that] of smell [4]), it is throughout motivated by one concern: namely, to show how, and under what influences psychological subject matter can assume a variety of social forms which are themselves reducible to that archtypical relativist category —viz., that of *reciprocity* in the interaction between individuals.

A sociology conceived of in this way shares with all other exact sciences—moral, political-economic, historical—the fact of having two boundaries with philosophy: viz., a frontier where it begins and a frontier where it leaves off. Of these two philosophical domains which border sociology as an exact science,

> . . . one concerns the conditions, the basic concepts, and the hypotheses of a particular piece of research. These cannot be said to be contained only in that research for they are the necessary conditions for it. Philosophy is utilized in a second way when the particular piece of research is raised to a level of generalization and synthesis which puts it in contact with concepts and problems which have no place either in experience or in completely objective knowledge. The first domain is that of the epistemology, and the second that of the metaphysics of sociology. The latter presents two problems (which are usually, and with reason, confused in everyday thought). The unsatisfactory fragmentary nature of piecemeal knowledge, combined with the poverty of the generalizations and truths which can be derived from it, tend to lead to a reliance on speculation as the means of giving them greater significance: and along with this tendency goes the inclination to formulate a unifying system in order to make up for the contradictions in, and lack of cohesion among, the fragments of piecemeal knowledge. Side by side with this metaphysical inclination (the direction of which is determined by the state of knowledge) comes another (which is directed by another dimension of reality) in which is invested the metaphysical significance of the subject matter. It is this to which we refer when we talk about the *direction* or the *end,* or about the *absolute*

[4] *Ibid.,* pp. 646-65.

substance underlying all relative phenomena, or about *value* or *religious significance*. In relation to society this problem gives rise to such questions as: Is society the goal of human existence or is it a means for the individual? Does it help him? Or, conversely, does it hinder him? Is society acting optimally when it simply maintains itself? Or when it facilitates the realization of some objective good? Or when it inculcates moral qualities in the individual? Can one draw an analogy between the stages of societal development and the cosmic processes, in the sense that the social relations of man must be seen as premised on a general rhythm or form which, while in itself alien to particular phenomena, is the basis of these, and is equally impartial in its control over the essential forces of material reality? In sum, can society be said to possess a metaphysical or religious meaning, or is such a thing reserved for individual souls only?[5]

These are essentially philosophical questions which relate to social philosophy rather than to sociology.

In truth *Soziologie* does not answer these questions. All Simmel gives, at the very most, are some fragmentary outlines in various journals. In these he defines his conception of the unity of life. . . . However, in recompense, Simmel does offer, in *Soziologie,* some very important statements on the theory of sociological knowledge. These statements, which are concerned with the philosophical domain of sociology rather than with sociology as an "exact" science, provide a definition of Simmelian sociology and serve to distinguish it from the French school. It is important to offer a succinct analysis of these formulations.

The theoretical problem posed by sociological knowledge is: How, in general, is society possible? It is true that one might be tempted to turn to history for an answer to this problem, but history can in no way account for the origin of the societal tie. Simmel uses an idea with which Auguste Comte was very taken, and shows, quite easily, that society could not have originated in an initial conviction as to its utility because such a conviction is of necessity the product of a long social evolution: i.e., the idea that social action is more effective than individual action could only have been arrived at a posteriori. This means that, if in fact there are any necessary preconditions for the existence of society, then

---

[5] *Ibid.,* pp. 25-26.

they must be discovered through a priori reasoning, and this involves, not the historian, but the philosopher as theoretician of knowledge. All the same, in spite of formal similarities, it is not possible to equate the question "How is society possible?" with the seemingly analogous problem posed by Kant: i.e., "How is nature possible?" Kant's solution cannot be applied to the sociological problem—and, for a variety of reasons, it would not be enough to rely on the synthetic function of the categories of knowledge.

The unity of society is not of the same order as the unity of nature. The unity of nature is the result of the activity of the observer who effects unity by means of separate and various categories of apperception—i.e., with the aid of a perceptual schema. The unity of society is independent of the synthesizing activity of the observer. It is effected directly and spontaneously by the action of the social elements themselves entering into a reciprocity of interaction. Furthermore, the quality of the relations which are established among, and which unify, the members of the social body are distinguished from those which unify the physical world in that while the latter is the world of juxtaposition, the former is the world of living complementarity. Finally, if one puts oneself in the position of the observer, it is clear that the unity which our perceptions can effect in the physical world is much narrower than that which we can effect in the social world. This is a result of the comparative simplicity of physical reality, which is composed of a relatively small number of homogeneous and impersonal elements which obey general laws, while society, on the other hand, is composed of a multitude of individual elements which are heterogeneous and irreducible. In effect, natural objects differ from the elements of the social body in that they exist only through our representation of them, while the latter—i.e., individuals—seem to us to have an existence independent of our representations. And this existence is as absolute and unconditional as is our own. If society *is* our representation, it is not so in the same way as is nature. The problem then becomes one of finding out, first, how we can treat other individuals as objects of analysis without ceasing to recognize that they have an existence independent of us and that in some ways they exist as objects in and of themselves, and, second, how we can envisage them as members, as such, of the society of which we are also part. This transformation of others from being objects in themselves to being objects of our representation and members of society is clearly dependent upon the use of categories, which are the purely a priori conditions of social knowledge.

Simmel sees three principal categories.

The first has already been defined in *Probleme der Geschichtsphilosophie* as one of the a priori's which determine the nature of historical research. It is the impossibility of ever possessing totally adequate knowledge of other individuals—i.e., of understanding them in those aspects which make them different from us. Thus, since we are forced to content ourselves with a fragmentary representation, we are led to generalize the traits which we have established empirically by putting them into a priori categories—*class, profession, party,* and so on. We come to know the individual through these general concepts—i.e., as a member of a class, or of a profession, or of a party, and we postulate this identity as his essential nature. By abstraction we limit, and by generalization we extend, the representation which we have of his individuality. The result of this is the denial of the individual because our methodology is such as to be unable to represent what is essentially irreducible in the individual. Simmel's formulation seems to be the opposite of Schopenhauer's. To Schopenhauer the individual is not real but is, rather, a construct of our representations, which therefore falsify reality. According to Simmel (and here he expands on one of the themes on which he was most insistent in the *Probleme der Geschichtsphilosophie*), the individual is of the essence of reality, and social thought—being suprapersonal, abstract, and general—is valid only because our representations are so inadequate and because of their pragmatic utility. This is the only justification for the use of concepts. This position of Simmel's emphasizes once again the clash between his sociological thought and that of Durkheim's school. The difference is both between nominalism and realism and between criticism and dogmatism.

The second category of sociological knowledge is based on the notion that social life does not incorporate the individual in his entirety, but that each individual preserves a section of his personality which is his own alone. This constitutes, so to speak, his private property. It remains quite irreducible; it is extrasocial and persists

side by side with those segments of his personality which engage him
in society as a member of such and such a social group. This concept
is clearly the theoretical complement of the first. It limits itself to
postulating the existence of a *foro interno,* of something in and of
itself, and thus provides a notion which the first category could not
contain. At the same time, it preserves the franchise of psychology
and history side by side with that of sociology. Moreover, in practice
the subject matters of the two categories are in incessant interaction.
The extra social self maintains a reciprocity of interaction with the
social self (the extrasocial self constituting the result of social influences; the social self devoting itself to directing the reaction of
the individual to those influences). The very real and profound
unity of the individual conforms to the basic Simmelian principle
of relativity when it is seen as being founded on this reciprocity of
ongoing action.

Finally, the third category—which is a synthesis of the first two
—concerns the inequality of social elements (unequal that is, not
in their worth but in their content and in their destiny). Because
of this inequality it would seem that each social element—i.e., each
individual—participates in society by playing a particular role to
which he is destined. Individual life (as defined by the second category) enters into contact with social life (as defined in the first
category). Society is fully developed and socialization is complete
only when the extrasocial life of the individual is fully integrated
with the social body of which he is part. This integration would
result in a perfect society (all moral or eudemonistic senses of the
word *perfect* being excised), but it seems that it would be possible
only in the event that the individual comes to accept the necessity
of putting himself in the role for which he was made. From this it
follows that socialization cannot be held to be a simple matter of
the net effect of a multiplicity of efficient causes, but as rather a goal
of the conscious individual—the causal sequence which eventuated
in the establishment of society transforms itself into a teleological
sequence. From now on, society appears as an environment in which
each individual finds an already prepared place which determines
the role he is to play. The interactions whose play constitutes the
web of social life are realized inside this teleological sequence—i.e.,
in that complementarity of individual rights and social duties

which is the ultimate reciprocity guaranteeing both individual autonomy and the conservation and progress of society. This complementarity and reciprocity constitute the fundamental law of civilized, democratic societies. When compared to the sociology of the Durkheimian school—which, it can be claimed with some truth, ascribes social reality only to undifferentiated and passive masses, or to prehistoric hordes, to primitive epochs, or to atrophied and decadent societies—it seems that Simmelian sociology has the great merit of being applicable to modern societies in which the individual is both legislator and citizen.

This is, in outline, Simmel's conception of sociology. Its essential distinguishing mark lies in its philosophical nature. Although it is —or, rather, because it is—the subject matter of an exact and positive science, social reality, like all other dimensions of reality, is embedded in philosophy. It is involved in philosophy in two different ways. First, because theoretical elaboration is necessary for the representation of social life; and, second, because—over and above positive knowledge—there is room for speculation relinking the social with the unity of life. And over and above all is a fact that, in the innermost part of the scientific study of society, one discovers the dominance of philosophical concepts whose application extends well beyond society. The sociology of Simmel is very clearly governed and directed by his relativist point of view, in particular by the notion of the complementarity and reciprocity of action—a notion which has already been applied in all other scientific disciplines. To Simmel the establishment of sociology as an independent, positive science in no way means the end of philosophy—on the contrary, for the theory of knowledge and of metaphysics retains all their prerogatives by virtue of their connection with this new science. It is this fact which is the source of the difference between the Simmelian and the contemporary positivist conceptions of sociology. It would appear that contemporary positivist sociology is too apt to deny the claim of philosophy to have a function and too eager to subsume it under scientific technique.

# PART THREE

# CURRENT APPRAISALS
# OF SIMMEL'S WORK

THE ESSAYS IN this section aim to acquaint the reader with some of the current appraisals of Georg Simmel's thought. F. H. Tenbruck, who now teaches at the University of Frankfort (after having spent a number of years in the United States), re-examines the notion of formal sociology as developed by Georg Simmel. This essay should go a long way in dispelling misconceptions of Simmel's approach and in elucidating the import of his contribution to sociological method.

Donald N. Levine, who teaches at the University of Chicago, codifies Simmel's sociological contributions by subsuming them under three major categories: *social processes, social types,* and *developmental patterns.* He then discusses in some detail a few strategic problems in Simmel's work by focusing attention upon his writings on fashion, aristocracy, social differentiation, and freedom.

Rudolf Heberle, of Louisiana State University, elucidates Simmel's method from still another vantage point. His profound knowledge of German sociological tradition allows him to place Simmel's work in the context of German discussions as to the proper method of sociology.

Rudolf H. Weingartner, who teaches philosophy at San Francisco State College, earned his doctorate in philosophy at Columbia University with a thesis on "Experience and Culture: The Philosophy of Georg Simmel." The chapter from this work reprinted here clarifies Simmel's approach to culture and his dialectical view of *The Tragedy of Culture.*

Shorter excerpts from the work of Albert Salomon, of The New

School of Social Research, and of the French sociologist Raymond Aron further clarify Simmel's view of the alienative aspects of culture by focusing upon his work on the functions of money.

Finally, Pitrim A. Sorokin, dean of American sociology, contributes a characteristically abrasive and astringent critique of Simmel's method.

# ONE

# FORMAL SOCIOLOGY

### F. H. TENBRUCK

. . . IF FORMS and contents constitute an inseparable entity in reality, the problem arises of how the forms can be studied. Simmel discusses this methodological problem in his program.[1] His first point in this discussion is that there exists, at present, no teachable method, no set of rules, for separating form from content. His second point is to recommend the use of what might be called the method of comparison: he suggests the comparative study of the forms in complexes of widely different content. Our interest here is not in either of these points but in his third and basic thesis: that the forms must be "abstracted" from reality.

It is at this point that what we have called the formalistic interpretation of Simmel's sociology launched its attack, led conspicuously and effectively by Sorokin. In Sorokin's view, the program of Simmel's formal sociology must result in "a purely scholastic and dead science, a kind of almost useless catalog of human relations."[2] It "studies the most general characteristics of social phenomena."[3] Another critic, Abel, writes: "Form is identical then with the generalized aspects of society."[4] This interpretation which sees formal

From Kurt H. Wolff (ed.), *Georg Simmel, 1858-1918: A Collection of Essays, with Translations and a Bibliography* (Columbus, Ohio: Ohio State University Press, 1959). Copyright © 1959 by the Ohio State University Press. Reprinted by permission of the author, the editor, and the publisher.

[1] Georg Simmel, *Soziologie* (Leipzig: Duncker und Humblot, 1908), pp. 11-13.

[2] Pitirim Sorokin, *Contemporary Sociological Theories* (New York and London: Harper & Row, Publishers, 1928). Cf. Raymond Aron, *German Sociology* (London: William Heinemann, Ltd., 1957).

[3] Sorokin, *op. cit.*, p. 501.

[4] Theodore Abel, *Systematic Sociology in Germany* (New York: Columbia University Press, 1929), p. 27; cf. p. 30.

sociology as a classificatory and merely analytic science is based on Simmel's assertions that the forms must be "abstracted" from reality. And the belief that they are merely abstract and generalized aspects must inevitably result in the standard reproach that Simmel's program places undue limitations on sociology that cut from it "its other more vital parts." [5]

However, Simmel is not understood by such hasty interpretation. When he speaks of abstracting the forms of sociation from reality, he does not plead for the establishment of categories of a high degree of abstractness (all concepts are, of course, abstract in varying degrees). His emphasis is not on the abstract character of the forms of sociation but on the process of abstracting them. It is this which poses a peculiar problem. The forms inhere in the totality of reality. They have no separate existence. How, then, can they be studied?

Simmel not only admits that the content often or always modifies the forms of sociation,[6] he explicitly postulates that "the historical facts which guarantee the actuality of the defined societal forms must be cited in their totality." [7] Forms can be demonstrated only in an arrangement of contents, the "synopsis" of which makes them perceptible. Abstraction for Simmel is not—it could not be—abstraction from content-*phenomena,* in which the forms inhere and through which alone they can be set forth, but abstraction from a content-*perspective.* He is anxious to warn us against the formalistic misunderstanding when he points out that forms of sociation must be considered in their concrete realizations, rather than on the basis of the "general" characteristics which their contents manifest.[8] The forms are by no means generalizations which retain only the most common characteristics of all contents. Science has long since developed teachable methods of studying them in this sense. In abstracting forms, one does not simply disregard the noncommon elements in the contents in order to arrive at the most general, but rather empty and "formal," characteristics. Forms are not general concepts arrived at by generalization and abstraction, and formal sociology

---

[5] Sorokin, *op. cit.,* p. 313.

[6] See *Soziologie, op. cit.,* pp. 8, 10, 451.

[7] *Ibid.,* p. 12 (Small, *op. cit.,* p. 307; cf. the statement on p. 304 that the form is "actualized through its contents"). [Small's translation of Simmel's "The Problem of Sociology," *American Journal of Sociology,* XV (1909), pp. 310-336.]

[8] *Soziologie, op. cit.,* p. 10 (Small, *op cit.,* p. 304).

is not the analysis of such general concepts. *Abstracting* must be understood in the radical sense of extracting or extricating from reality something which is not a directly observable and common element in it. In abstracting the forms of sociation, the wealth of phenomena is no more disregarded or repressed than in any other science.

Simmel's program does not rule out content. All it asks is that reality be viewed, not with regard to inherent content, but with regard to its forms. Sociology is offered as the study of the entire realm of sociocultural phenomena; but it must relate them to its proper object: that is, the forms of sociation. The scope of sociology, as a special social science, is in no way limited. It gets its name, not from a restriction of its material, but from the perspective applied to it. It may draw on all facts, not adding them up for what they are worth within the frames of other fields (psychology and economics, for example), but extracting from them their social forms: "Not its object but its manner of contemplation, the peculiar abstraction which it performs, differentiates it from the other historico social sciences." [9] In his concrete investigations, Simmel does practice the method he designed in his program, and he does not overstep any of the fictitious limitations which the formalistic misunderstanding has read into this program.

There is another aspect which must be mentioned. For Simmel, no true theory of form seemed feasible: "There is never in existence 'society' in an absolute sense . . . but merely particular species of the same." [10] Sociology is the study of the forms, but it cannot study form per se. Later we shall touch on the broader significance of this statement. It suffices here to say that the lack of rigor in Simmel's sociology is partly a consequence of his dismissal of a theory of form. Lacking such a theory, he could set forth the general meaning of form only by analogy.

In spite of Simmel's fundamental unity of thought and a remotely familiar note struck by some of his arguments, modern readers may find formal sociology something of an archaism. One reason for this may be that the terminology of the social sciences has changed

[9] Small, *op. cit.*, p. 301 (*Soziologie, op. cit.*, p. 8).
[10] Small, *op. cit.*, p. 303 (*Soziologie, op. cit.*, p. 10).

with the advances that have been made since Simmel wrote. Terminologies have a way of absorbing the attention of people to such a degree that even the truly imaginative find it hard to recognize statements for what they are once their apparel has been changed. It is necessary, therefore, to relate Simmel's arguments to modern sociology—not to any particular system or problem, but to the field in general—in such a way as to enable a contemporary reader to realize how extremely modern Simmel's approach is. That quality which makes reading Simmel such a captivating and fascinating experience may then be less puzzling.

The basic problems of formal sociology are still with us. One such problem is to reach an understanding of social action. Simmel pointed out that, sociologically, interaction is more than the sum of actors pursuing their individual goals while being influenced by such favorable or unfavorable moments as the action-systems of other actors may represent. Social action contains some unity of the actors. Simmel's argument is fully alive in Florian Znaniecki's approach to social action:

> A real objective social connection between two agents, not merely between two actions, is made only when those agents rise above the one-sidedness of their separate points of view as agents, so as to create together a mutuality of experience and activity which did not exist originally.[11]

The second essential point in formal sociology—the discrimination between form and content as two different aspects of action—is discussed in Talcott Parsons' theory of social action:

> The scheme, that is relative to the units of action and interaction, is a *relational* scheme. It analyzes the structure and processes of the systems built up by the relations of such units to their situations, including other units. It is not as such concerned with the *internal* structure of the units except so far as this directly bears on the relational system.[12]

Even more pointedly, he says:

[11] Florian Znaniecki, *Social Actions* (New York: Farrar, Straus & Company, 1936), p. 121.

[12] Talcott Parsons, *The Social System* (New York: The Free Press of Glencoe, Inc., 1951), p. 4.

In the most general sense the "need-disposition" system of the individual actor seems to have two most primary or elementary aspects which may be called the *gratificational* aspect and the *orientational* aspect. The first concerns the "content" of his interchange with the object world, *what* he gets out of his interaction with it, and what its "costs" to him are. The second concerns the *how* of his relation to the object world, the patterns or ways in which his relations to it are organized.[13]

Whatever differences may exist between formal sociology and Parsons' system otherwise, the distinction he draws here between the two aspects coincides in essence with Simmel's distinction between content and form.

It can, indeed, be maintained "that the problems raised by men like Simmel and Durkheim are still far from settled." [14] But there is a still more fundamental way in which Simmel's approach can be considered as being part of modern sociology. Kurt H. Wolff says of Simmel's system: "It is close to the modern concern with 'social structure.' " [15] Modern sociology has developed an elaborate system of concepts for describing social structure in general; the concepts of *status, role, typical expectations, typical actions,* and *norms* are foremost among these. In principle, the forms of sociation are specific roles, statuses, and norms, viewed as reciprocities and as they occur in historical complexes. Conversely, the theory of social structure is merely a theory of form per se.

As explained above, Simmel declared that such a theory was impossible on the ground that only specific forms exist, not form as such. In describing specific forms, he made extensive use of such concepts as *role, position,* and *norm;* but having denied the possibility of a general theory of form, he failed to perceive the significance of these concepts for a general theory of social structure and was forced to introduce his program for a study of the structure of society (in the broadest sense) by analogy, rather than by systematic conceptualization. Modern sociology must not overlook the fact that

[13] *Ibid.,* p. 7.
[14] Reinhard Bendix, "Max Weber's Interpretation of Conduct and History," *American Journal of Sociology,* LI (1946), 518.
[15] Kurt H. Wolff (ed.), *The Sociology of Georg Simmel* (New York: The Free Press of Glencoe, Inc., 1950). Cf. Rudolf Heberle, "The Sociology of Georg Simmel," in Harry Elmer Barnes (ed.), *An Introduction to the History of Sociology* (Chicago: The University of Chicago Press, 1948).

Simmel was the first to apprehend and point to this peculiar "layer" or "aspect" of social reality. It continues to pay silent tribute to formal sociology by designating social structure as the principal object of sociology. Whether it deals with institutions or processes, the frame of reference is always structure; the study is made in terms of patterns of reciprocal behavior—roles, statuses, and norms. The "limitation" which Simmel placed on sociology has, in fact, been widely accepted.

Occasionally, Simmel speaks of "pure" forms of sociation. He uses this term—or, more often, various other terms containing the word *pure*—to refer to a complex idea which represents an important element—perhaps even the central element—of Simmel's thought.[16] An inarticulate formulation of his idea of pure forms appears in the programmatic essay: "This object, abstracted from reality, may be viewed . . . with reference to such laws, indifferent toward their realization in time and space, as reside purely in the objective structure of its elements." [17] Clarification of this peculiar statement may be found in the essay "Superordination and Subordination." In an attempt to justify an earlier theorem that certain forms of superordination go together with "leveling," he writes:

> It need hardly be mentioned that *leveling* must always be understood here as a wholly relative tendency with very limited possibilities of realization. A basic science of the forms of society must present concepts and concept complexes in a purity and abstract completeness which are never shown by the historical realizations of their contents. Yet sociological understanding aims at grasping the fundamental concept of sociation in its particular significances and formations; it aims at analyzing phenomenal complexes into their minute factors to the point of approaching inductive regularities. It can do so only through the auxiliary construction of, so to speak, absolute lines and figures which in actual social life are found only as beginnings and fragments, as

---

[16] In "Fundamental Problems of Sociology" (contained in Wolff, *op. cit.*, pp. 1-84), the term *pure forms* has been divested of most of this earlier meaning and serves a different purpose. Simmel's silence on the problem of pure concepts may be interpreted as a reluctance to pursue his theory of pure concepts after Max Weber had become identified with the method of ideal-types. In any case, his work of later years shows that he had not changed his fundamental position on the matter.

[17] *Soziologie, op. cit.*, p. 10 (Small, *op. cit.*, p. 305).

partial realizations that are constantly interrupted and modified. In every single social-historical configuration, there operates a number of reciprocities among the elements, which can probably never wholly be enumerated. . . . Sociological cognition so transforms historical phenomena that their unity is decomposed into a number of concepts and syntheses which are defined in a purely one-sided manner and which run, as it were, in a straight line. As a rule, one of these catches the main characteristic of the historical phenomenon under analysis. By bending and limiting each other mutually, all of them together project its image with increasing exactness upon the new plane of abstraction.[18]

Now the idea is clear: the forms, which are found in reality, are not "pure" forms. A multitude of forms are present in every social situation as a historical phenomenon, and each limits the realization of the other. Consequently, only "distorted" forms can be discovered in reality. This situation urgently poses the question: "How, this being the case, can sociology ever learn about the 'pure' forms?" Simmel answers that it must exaggerate certain characteristics of the historical phenomenon to the point where they become "absolute lines and figures," so that they can be defined "in a purely one-sided manner." This method, which was heralded by the programmatic essay, is no longer strictly empirical-inductive. Although it starts with the "social-historical reality," it must finally rely on something else for selecting and exaggerating features of that reality in order to bring out the inherent structural order of the elements involved. Forms, then, are not merely generalized aspects of "observed" reality and must not be mistaken for general, inductive concepts—notwithstanding their relation to reality. Far from merely mirroring reality, they also render it intelligible to us. The relations among the elements have an "evidence" of their own, and, consequently, their validity does not depend on how often they have found expression in historical reality. In a way, the idea finds a mature expression in the essay that followed "Superordination and Subordination." In "The Persistence of Social Groups," Simmel writes: "It is inevitable that sociology, as an abstract science, can never exhaust the full wealth and complexity of historical reality by the typical relations which it describes." [19] Simmel follows this

---

[18] Wolff, *op. cit.*, p. 200 (*Soziologie, op. cit.*, pp. 113 f.).
[19] *Soziologie, op. cit.*, p. 418 n. Cf. n. 23, below.

passage with the reassertion that the typical relations which sociology ascertains are not of the strictly general, inductive kind, and ends by characterizing sociology as a "cognition of typical laws." [20]

There can be little doubt that here is the distinct notion of what has become known as the *ideal-type*. Max Weber could not and did not claim to be the first to employ ideal-types, but he is usually given credit for being the first to delineate the true character of the concept and—on the basis of his delineation—to recommend its use in sociology and other branches of the human studies.[21] His methodological treatment of ideal-types is more elaborate, careful, specific, and complete than Simmel's discussions of pure forms. Weber distinguishes between merely heuristic ideal-types and those designed to capture the actual orientations of people, and he warns against the reification of the heuristic concepts. In substance, however, his undertaking is hardly larger than Simmel's, for Simmel asserts that sociology needs concepts which are abstracted from features of historical reality and exaggerated in certain respects so as to bring out configurations and relations which underlie reality but are not fully actualized in it. Such concepts limit one another's actualizations; they carry some intrinsic evidence of their own and are not automatically invalidated by incongruous facts; and they are not simply generalized aspects of reality, although they have an inductive basis. Both Simmel and Weber believe that no strictly logical and teachable method for developing such concepts can be devised.[22]

It appears that the idea of "pure" concepts evolved throughout

[20] *Ibid.*, p. 418.

[21] In his first programmatic essay, "Die Objektivität sozialwissenschaftlicher und sozialpolitischer Erkenntnis," *Archiv für Sozialwissenschaft und Sozialpolitik,* XIX (1904), 22-87. For a translation, see Edward A. Shils and Henry A. Finch (eds.), *Max Weber on the Methodology of the Social Sciences* (New York: The Free Press of Glencoe, Inc., 1949), pp. 50-112. Cf. Talcott Parsons, "The Contribution of Max Weber," in Barnes, *op. cit.*, p. 291.

[22] Weber's positions on these matters can be seen in the essays "Die Objektivität sozialwissenschaftlicher und sozialpolitischer Erkenntnis" and "Über einige Kategorien der verstehenden Soziologie," *Logos,* IV (1913). For his discussion of the idea that the forms limit one another's actualizations, see Max Weber, *Gesammelte Aufsätze zur Religionssoziologie* (Tübingen: J. C. B. Mohr [Paul Siebeck], 1920), I, 273, 424 ff. See also Max Weber, *Gesammelte Aufsätze zur Wissenschaftslehre* (Tübingen: J. C. B. Mohr [Paul Siebeck], 1922), p. 521.

the course of Simmel's sociological work.[23] It occupies a central position in "The Persistence of Social Groups" and continues to unfold and grow from that point on. In *Philosophie des Geldes*, which Weber read shortly before he wrote his own first programmatic essay,[24] Simmel anticipates the method of the entire book in the Preface and later states it explicitly:

> Innumerable times, we form our concepts of objects in such a manner that experience can show no equivalent of their pure and absolute character; they gain an empirical form only in being weakened and limited by opposing concepts. . . . This peculiar method of exaggerating and reducing concepts yields knowledge of the world which is commensurate with our mode of cognition. . . . Our intellect can grasp reality only by limitations of pure concepts which, no matter how far they deviate from reality, prove their legitimacy by the service they render for the interpretation of it.[25]

When Simmel finally undertook a somewhat methodological treatment of this central idea, he did so in his customarily oblique way, and, moreover, he immersed it in a comprehensive analysis of history.[26] At the time, Weber had just published his own outline of ideal-types in "Die Objektivität sozialwissenschaftlicher und sozialpolitischer Erkenntnis."

It might be argued that Weber would never have considered applying the method of ideal-types to such a topic as money. This

[23] Simmel's *Soziologie* is, in substance, a collection of articles previously published during the period from 1890 to 1907. Not having access to all of his essays in their original versions, I cannot go beyond establishing the fact that Simmel had developed the nucleus of a theory of pure concepts prior to Weber's first outline of ideal-types. As far as I can ascertain now, the idea of pure concepts is entirely missing in Simmel's writings before 1896-97. At least, the translations of the early drafts of his essays which appeared in American journals show no clear understanding of the character of sociology as described by idealtypes, even though his insistence on "the abstract character of sociology" may have to be interpreted in light of a later passage from "The Persistence of Social Groups," *American Journal of Sociology*, III (1898), 691 n., where the nucleus of the idea of pure concepts is clearly and definitely recognizable.
[24] H. H. Gerth and C. Wright Mills (eds.), *From Max Weber: Essays in Sociology* (New York: Oxford University Press, Inc., 1946), p. 14.
[25] Georg Simmel, *Philosophie des Geldes* (Leipzig: Duncker und Humblot, 1900), p. 135. See also p. 552 and *passim*.
[26] Georg Simmel, *Die Probleme der Geschichtsphilosophie* (2nd rev. ed., Duncker und Humblot, 1905).

is true enough. Weber narrowed the range of application of ideal-types to historically circumscribed phenomena, and in doing so he may have lodged an implicit criticism of Simmel, particularly of his laxity in the use of terminology. But this is, at least partially, a deceptive summary of the situation. By the time he wrote *Philosophie des Geldes*, Simmel had become accustomed to referring to historically circumscribed phenomena by means of pure concepts. When he speaks of "the objective spirit of modern marriage" [27] and of "the metropolitan type of individuality" or "metropolitan man," [28] he is well aware of using such concepts. Furthermore, Weber never actually restricted the method of ideal-types to the characterization of unique historical complexes, but seems to have planned and used it to ascertain functional laws and relations.[29] Therefore, though there are differences, the range of application of pure concepts is basically and systematically identical in both Simmel's formal and Weber's *verstehende* sociology.

The community of ideas between Simmel and Weber is not confined to their agreement concerning the pure concepts. In spite of conspicuous differences in style, thought, terminology, and presentation, and differences in degrees of precision, explicitness, and elaboration, the fundamental understandings and frames of reference of formal and *verstehende* sociology are very similar—perhaps, identical. It has been noticed that Weber's types of social action have their counterpart in formal sociology.[30] In addition, Weber's definition of *social action*[31] exhibits the understanding of function which Simmel had introduced in his idea of interaction. And, like Simmel, Weber sees the regularities of behavior rooted in reciprocal orientations.[32] Like Simmel, he is anxious to exclude all merely identical behavior ("parallel," "statistical" phenomena)[33] from social

[27] *Philosophie des Geldes, op. cit.*, p. 497. Cf. *Soziologie, op. cit.*, p. 270.

[28] Wolff, *op. cit.*, pp. 409, 411.

[29] See Weber, *Gesammelte Aufsätze zur Wissenschaftslehre, op. cit.*, p. 520, and Alexander von Schelting, *Max Webers Wissenschaftslehre* (Tübingen: J. C. B. Mohr [Paul Siebeck], 1934).

[30] Albert Salomon, "German Sociology," in Georges Gurvitch and Wilbert E. Moore (eds.), *Twentieth Century Sociology* (New York: Philosophical Library, Inc., 1945).

[31] Weber, *Gesammelte Aufsätze zur Wissenschaftslehre, op. cit.*, pp. 405 ff.

[32] *Ibid.*, pp. 408, 428.

[33] *Ibid.*, p. 430.

action. Like Simmel, he frees sociology from psychology.[34] The principal identity of viewpoint can be found in Weber's repeated comments that the same social action may be performed by various actors for entirely different reasons—this is the very argument on which Simmel had based his distinction between form and content.[35]

Aside from his concrete investigations, Weber's contributions to sociology appear to lie in his discriminating systematization and conceptualization, and in the establishment of operational criteria, rather than in the development of new basic understandings. Among other things, the introduction of such concepts as *chances* or *expectations,* together with the systematic and controlled use of them, and the investigation of the connections between *verstehen* and causal analysis, mark Weber's achievements in the field of methodology; and from them, sociology—including his own concrete investigations—has profited enormously. What Simmel had deemed impossible, a theory of form in general, emerged in Weber's work.

Whatever the relations between the two men may have been, they should be placed in historical perspective, and should be related, above all, to the issue which Heinrich Rickert, more than anybody else, had forced on German science at the turn of the century. Rickert's rigid belief that only the natural sciences were capable of ascertaining laws was widely shared, and, in consequence of it, the "cultural" sciences were limited to the treatment of unique

[34] *Ibid.,* pp. 408, 428, 430, 436. Simmel's and Weber's attempts to exclude psychology (including social psychology) from sociological analysis must be read in light of what they understood psychology to be and what psychology was at the time. This opposition to psychology on the part of Simmel does not necessarily conflict with the views of some interpreters who regard his sociology as a variety of social psychology.

[35] *Ibid.,* pp. 404, 436, *passim.* As a matter of fact, the similarities between Simmel and Weber go much further than this; and I am not referring to those parts of Simmel's sociology—his view of differentiation, for example—which reflect, directly or indirectly, trends and assumptions common among German scholars at the time. Although we find this very same idea of differentiation in Weber, both men were here only participants in a broad stream of current thought. However, it is quite obvious that Weber's "Über einige Kategorien der verstehenden Soziolgie" is strongly influenced by Simmel. In fact, Sections V and VI of this paper are hardly more than a systematization of Simmel's basic understandings and terminology; they freely borrow some of Simmel's characteristic teachings, such as that concerning conflict.

historical phenomena. This limitation excluded any generalizing sociology from their ranks. In view of this historical context, it seems strange that Weber so openly acknowledged his indebtedness to Rickert, whereas his references to "my friend Simmel" [36] are rather perfunctory or dilatory, often fastening on minor points in Simmel's works.[37] It could be that Weber's sense of meticulous scholarship and his distaste for anything that lacked precision or was reminiscent of intuition led him to underestimate Simmel's value to systematic sociology.[38] Unfortunately, Weber's tribute to Rickert placed him in opposition to Simmel and, moreover, to sociology. There could be no mistaking this at a time when one issue kept all German scholars under its spell. Simmel, in open defiance of the dichotomy which Rickert and others had imposed on the entire realm of German scholarship—the rigorous distinction between natural (generalizing) and "cultural" (individualizing) sciences, a distinction which made sociology a historical discipline— had written:

> If the alternative to which nowadays every science is put is whether it aims at finding eternally valid laws or at describing and understanding single historically real processes, . . . then the necessity of a decision does not apply to the problem as here posed.[39]

This leads directly to the later characterization of sociology as the "cognition of typical laws."

However, in spite of his recurrent recognition of Rickert's system, Weber assumed the very position taken by Simmel. Sociology was expected to find typical relations. Indeed, Weber's thought has, at best, a thin veneer of Rickert's philosophy; and Rickert himself,

[36] Gerth and Mills, op. cit., p. 115.

[37] See the many references to Simmel, mostly in footnotes, throughout Gesammelte Aufsätze zur Wissenschaftslehre. For an instance of the dilatory character of these references, see p. 97. For an example of Weber's criticism of irrelevant points, see p. 76, where he attacks a statement of Simmel's, the true significance of which he is unaware because he has disregarded the context in which it is made.

[38] See Weber, Gesammelte Aufsätze zur Wissenschaftslehre, op. cit., p. 403, n. 1. See also Max Weber, Grundriss der Sozialökonomik, III. Abteilung: Wirtschaft und Gesellschaft (Tübingen: J. C. B. Mohr [Paul Siebeck], 1925), p. 1.

[39] Soziologie, op. cit., p. 10 (Small, op. cit., p. 305).

in spite of his efforts to show Weber's dependence on his philosophy, was forced to admit it eventually.[40]

As Simmel's sociology emerged in his series of papers, the term *forms* came more and more to stand for an ideal-type of reciprocal orientations. His terminology was changing. The word *Typus,* which he adopted as a synonym for *Form* in the late 1890's, occupies a prominent place in *Philosophie des Geldes;* and in his *Soziologie, Typus,* and *Formtypus* have largely replaced *Form.* This conception of forms as ideal-types implies a particular view of their ontological status, which sets them off distinctly from generalized and abstract concepts. Throughout his major sociological works—the two just mentioned and the 1905 edition of *Die Probleme der Geschichtsphilosophie*—Simmel vindicates the "dignity" of the forms of sociation.[41] In recurring statements, he extends their validity beyond the strictly empirical realm.

Simmel speaks of two aspects of the dignity of the forms. In the first, as explained in "The Persistence of Social Groups," it resides in the fact that forms are superior to individual existences and are not subject to individual wills because they persist while individuals come and go. This persistence of the forms and the irrelevance of the individuals involved in them do not result from some supra-individual force, but are accounted for by the nature of group interaction. Since they are operative in all members of a group, the reciprocities cannot be changed by them at will. There are other reasons, but their "dignity" is deceptive: they reflect only the individual's limitations and do not explain the persistence of the forms.[42]

Most of the time, however, when discussing this peculiar status of the forms, Simmel is referring to the second aspect, the authentic dignity, which lies in the "objective structure" of their elements. This structure is independent of its historical realizations.[43] Forms,

[40] Heinrich Rickert, *Die Grenzen der naturwissenschaftlichen Begriffsbildung* (Tübingen: J. C. B. Mohr [Paul Siebeck], 1929), pp. xxiii f., and Rickert, "Max Weber und seine Stellung zur Wissenschaft," *Logos,* XV (1926), 222-37.

[41] *Soziologie, op. cit.,* pp. 10, 422 f., 418 n., *passim.* Cf. *Geschichtsphilosophie, op. cit.,* p. 107 f.

[42] *Soziologie, op. cit.,* pp. 376 ff.

[43] See n. 41, above.

in this sense, represent typical laws. Certain elements go together: they "fit." These "objective" clusters can refer to simultaneous elements or to sequences of elements. To use an earlier example: in certain types of superordination, there exists a tendency toward "leveling." The absence of this tendency indicates that there is either an obstacle to the full realization of the ideal-type or a lack of other "typical" elements of the constellation, in which case a different type of superordination must be found to reveal the "fit" of the coexisting, essential elements.[44]

Although this may strike a modern reader as a philosophical— if not outright metaphysical and speculative—idea, it is nonetheless not wholly foreign to contemporary sociology. Max Weber, in spite of his insistence on causal analysis as a check on the meaningful relations of elements which are claimed to inhere in an ideal-type, urged sociology to derive the laws of social reality from "type-con-cepts"—that is, from constellations of elements whose "fit" can be demonstrated by their meanings.[45] The same principle, however, can also be found to underlie all functional approaches. If the ele-ments of social structure are not independent of each other, then it must be possible, within limits, to determine from a number of them something about the rest.

Simmel is not unaware of the limitations of this method. In his investigations he points out repeatedly that a given typical constel-lation of elements, though tending to go with certain other elements, may also be found with different ones, depending on which addi-tional phenomena in the situation may change the "functional" value and meaning of the elements. The "objective structure" of a form of sociation is always provisional; and for this reason he denies the status of natural laws to the "laws" inherent in the typical forms of sociation.[46]

What, then, is the ontological status of the forms of sociation? For the mature Simmel, they have come to mean typical clusters of reciprocal orientations whose "objective structure" rests on the affinity which the orientations possess by virtue of the meanings they

---

[44] Simmel sets forth this idea in terms of such concepts as *dualism* or *polarity*. Cf. *Soziologie, op. cit.*, pp. 536 f., 134, 188, 569, *passim*.

[45] Weber, *Gesammelte Aufsätze zur Wissenschaftslehre, op. cit.*, p. 520.

[46] *Soziologie, op. cit.*, p. 152, *passim*.

have for the actors. They are neither generalized aspects of social reality nor merely heuristic principles but are operative in the actors, as we saw before. As Simmel points out in the second chapter of the second edition of *Die Probleme der Geschichtsphilosophie,* they must not, on the other hand, be considered adequate causes of action. They have an empirical basis; but because of their inherent "objective structure," they must be given a status above that of merely empirical generalizations.

The characteristics of the forms may be presented in a summary statement as follows: Forms represent a specific "layer" of reality. Although they cannot—and are not meant to—account for interaction itself, they are operative in it; they account for its patterns. They exert constraint in the structuring of actions, but they do not do so only in that they are found directly operative in a social situation: if a form of sociation is certain elements-in-relation, then the recurrence of some of these elements must indicate the recurrence of the others, unless it can be demonstrated that some of the relevant conditions have changed and that, consequently, a different form of sociation is in question. In addition, if forms have an inherent tendency in time to result in certain new configurations, then a similar process will be repeated upon each occurrence of the initial form. In that they recurrently bring about typical situations and typical changes, forms provide a basis upon which predictions can be made.[47]

Boskoff is correct in writing that "the forms of sociation cannot be justly characterized as unreal, empty . . . for they are derived from an analysis of empirical phenomena."[48] But this must not lead to the belief that they are merely generalizations or heuristic concepts for the organization of data. Forms are reciprocal orientations which go with typical situations; and typical situations are obviously assumed to transcend, in their radical meaning, any particular culture—that is, no culture is entirely free to "define" typical situations. This constitutes, in the end, the "dignity" of the forms of

---

[47] The use of the forms for making predictions is limited. Historical laws cannot be derived from them; these must be treated on a different level, as we shall show below.

[48] Boskoff, "From Social Thought to Sociological Theory," in Howard Becker and Alvin Boskoff (eds.), *Modern Sociological Theory in Continuity and Change* (New York: The Dryden Press, 1957).

sociation; it is this that gives them a validity which is independent of their historical frequency.

There is an elusive, yet important, difference between formal sociology and the predominant contemporary sociology. The latter conceives of itself as the study of society, and society is explained, by and large, in terms of roles, statuses, and norms. Curiously enough, these specific roles, statuses, and norms are, in turn, explained in terms of society; they are acquired in the process of socialization and are made strong by rewards and punishments. The emphasis of modern sociology lies on this socialization into given roles. In a way, then, modern sociology is predominantly concerned with a description of the structure of society as a going and persisting phenomenon.[49] The individual appears largely as a mere functionary in society, for the structural pattern is conceived as a social system, and society, as such a system, is the object of investigation and the ultimate unit of reference.

By contrast, the prime object of investigation for Simmel is sociation. It is given priority over society in his system. According to Simmel, sociology cannot directly study society as a unit, as a social system, but must investigate the forms of sociation. Society is a composite of these forms of sociation,[50] and they must be understood in and by themselves, and not merely as functional ingredients of an inclusive system. It has been remarked that Simmel does not clearly distinguish between group and society.[51] This is not an oversight on his part. The distinction is incidental to an approach which makes the forms of sociation, rather than society as a social system, the object of analysis. In order to understand social reality,

[49] Although there is no intention of overlooking the many pioneering ventures which seek a comprehensive theory of society, capable of accounting for both its static and dynamic aspects, the reference here is specifically to the textbook literature.

[50] "There is never in existence 'society' in an absolute sense, i.e., of such a sort that all these particular phenomena would occur in accordance with 'society' as a presupposition; for there is no such thing as reciprocal influencing in an absolute sense but merely particular species of the same. With the occurrence of these species society also puts in an appearance. They are, however, neither the cause nor the consequence of society. They are themselves immediately society." Quoted from Small, *op. cit.*, p. 303 (*Soziologie, op. cit.*, p. 9). Cf. *Soziologie*, p. 5.

[51] Nicholas S. Timasheff, *Sociological Theory: Its Nature and Growth* (Garden City, N.Y.: Doubleday & Company, Inc., 1955).

we must not interpret phenomena as functional variables or as elements of a system, but must ascertain those basic possibilities of reciprocal orientation which underlie social reality and structure interaction. The forms of sociation stand in their own right and must be studied in their own right; they have independent force and meaning in and of themselves, even though their observable effect may be obscured by limitations inherent in the composite character of society. Simmel considers it fallacious to assume that

> . . . all these forms—hierarchies and corporations, competitions and forms of marriage, friendships and customs of sociability— . . . merely occur as moments in already existing societies. . . . This idea is prompted by the fact that in every known society a great number of such forms of union, that is, of sociation, are operative. Consequently, if a single one of these disappeared, "society" would still remain. . . . But if we eliminate in thought *all* these particular forms, no society remains.[52]

This approach may tend to minimize the effects which culture or society, as a system, has on all of its parts. On the other hand, it is a safeguard against any reification of society and, moreover, against the temptation to restrict sociological analysis to the description of how a social structure persists. In the delineation of its object of investigation, formal sociology heeds the fundamental problem of how forms originate. It matters little that Simmel provides no definitive answer when he explicitly deals with the question in "How Is Society Possible?" What is of real interest is that the choice of object makes formal sociology, in principle, immune to the predicament that plagues much of modern sociology—that is, the conspicuous cleavage between the theory of social structure and the theory of social change. Alvin Boskoff has recently pointed out the bewildering aspects of this situation.[53] The source of the dilemma does not lie in the fact that the concept of social structure as such eludes the understanding of the dynamics of social life, but in the fact that social structure is, in the main, conceived of as the mechanism for the persistence of groups and the transmission of culture. The theory of social structure has tended to become a theory of

---

[52] *Soziologie, op. cit.,* p. 8 (Small, *op. cit.,* p. 302).

[53] Boskoff, "Social Change: Major Problems in the Emergence of Theoretical and Research Foci," in Becker and Boskoff, *op. cit.,* pp. 260-302.

social statics, failing to explain social change or even systematically to allow for its possibility. In some textbooks, the cursory treatment of social change is found to relapse into a discourse on naïve common-sense concepts which beg the problem by locating the cause of change in, for example, "social movements," for which there can be no systematic accounting within a theory of social structure that is confined to the static aspect of society.

Formal sociology does not encounter these difficulties. Simmel knows of socialization and cultural learning; he is in no way blind to the fact that many forms of sociation are institutionalized. Fundamentally, however, sociation does not so much refer to those reciprocities which "society," in one way or another, inculcates in its members as to those which originate in interaction. Simmel urges sociology to consider the seemingly negligible forms of sociation, as they occur in everyday life, in addition to the crystallized and organized patterns of interaction. By this recommendation in the programmatic essay, he is not suggesting a merely quantitative extension of the field of investigation, and any interpretation of it as such misses an essential point.[54] For Simmel, these negligible forms have priority inasmuch as they retain what is spontaneous in sociation. His major emphasis lies on the process in which sociation emerges, not on that in which a given form of sociation persists. Forms represent society in its *status nascendi,* as Simmel put it, not in regard to its beginning in time but to the continuous spontaneity through which it is sustained.[55]

Forms develop in interaction. And this means not only that a form originates in the process of interaction and subsequently restrains and structures the actors' behavior, but also that the actors "add" elements to, or "subtract" elements from, established forms. For Simmel, the actors never lose this spontaneity, this influence on forms. The forms thus have a dual character, at once superior to the actors and subject to them. They operate on the actors, and the actors operate on them. This duality is particularly striking in Simmel's analyses of those forms in which the typical relations of

[54] See Floyd N. House, *The Development of Sociology* (New York and London: McGraw-Hill Book Company, Inc., 1936), p. 389. See also Heberle, *op. cit.,* p. 252.
[55] *Soziologie, op. cit.,* p. 15 (Small, *op. cit.,* p. 311).

the elements, and the typical tendencies inherent in them, are almost invariably based on the spontaneity of the actors, who are shown to adopt or drop practices and institutions for what seem to be reasons of their own. To illustrate by the example used earlier: leveling, as a tendency inherent in a specific form of sociation, rests on the desire of the superordinate to prevent the rise of groups that would challenge him. A minimum of attention in reading Simmel's analysis reveals that motives, interests, and so on, appear as the true moving forces.[56] However, in following their interests and motives, the individuals actually comply with the forms.

This dual character of the forms of sociation is deceptive. The form "rule-by-one," for example, contains, as a typical ingredient, the tendency toward leveling and can thus be said to compel the ruler to abide by it. But there is, of course, such a form only because, among other things, the ruler can understand that the situation demands it. It is possible for forms to operate on individual actors only because the actors "understand" the situation. Forms are the latent reciprocities of typical situations. And the "understanding" of a situation—that is, the grasping of its essential and typical features—is, for Simmel, not restricted to those situations which culture has revealed to the actors as typical. Formal sociology rests on the assumption that meaningful action can originate in the individuals. It is this assumption which allows for the peculiar understanding of society in which man is at once object and subject, an understanding of society which grasps it in its static and dynamic aspects at the same time.

[56] As far as I can see, no serious attempt has ever been made to follow the advice which Simmel offers on p. 13 of *Soziologie, op. cit.* Here he says that an understanding of his idea of formal sociology should be sought in his concrete investigations. What, actually, is the method he practices in them? What answer do they give to the inquiry concerning the "forces, relations, and forms" of sociation that he proposes on p. 8 of *Soziologie?* This article suggests an approach to a fuller understanding of formal sociology by drawing attention to the fact that, throughout his essays, Simmel presents the forms and their inherent tendencies as consequences of motives, or as modes of expression which are appropriate for certain ends. In the frame of reference of formal sociology, these motives must obviously be understood not as belonging to the individual action systems but as derived from typical situations. It is assumed that the actors possess certain reciprocal orientations, including motivations, which, regardless of the contents of their individual action systems, are among the inherent necessities of typical situations.

By the very nature of its approach, formal sociology has an affinity to the dynamic aspect of social reality. [Because] the component elements, the forms of sociation, are not viewed as variables of a given social system on which they are fundamentally dependent, society is not conceived of as an inert body seeking solely to maintain itself in the status quo. Forms express not only existing reciprocal orientations but also offer fundamental possibilities of social interactions as they originate, develop, and change. In this respect, they provide a basis for making predictions, and formal sociology seems close to being a full-fledged theory of social change.

Actually, however, the predictive value of the forms of sociation is limited. [Because] society is a composite phenomenon, historical reality is never exhausted by any specific form; a number of forms are always operative in reality and we cannot fully reconstruct reality as a combination of them.[57] Consequently, although the forms are instruments of prediction by virtue of their ontological status, their actual use as such is restricted. They cannot be applied to society as a whole, as a system, but only to specified aspects of it. If only one form were operative in society, we could predict actual social change. But not knowing precisely the relative contribution of any specific form, we can only assert that the presence of that form makes for a certain tendency which is part of the social situation. As Simmel usually puts it, the pure forms underlie social reality without ever being fully realized, [for] the various forms which make up this reality limit one another's actualizations. In formal sociology, *social change* means tendencies in specified aspects of society. Formal sociology is incompetent to deal with the problem of a change of society itself, a change of the whole system. It cannot be otherwise, for it refuses to regard society, as conceived of as such a system, as its proper object. . . .

[57] See *Soziologie, op. cit.,* p. 418; *Geschichtsphilosophie, op. cit.,* pp. 100, 102 ff.; and *Philosophie des Geldes, op. cit.,* p. 552.

# TWO

# SOME KEY PROBLEMS
# IN SIMMEL'S WORK

### DONALD N. LEVINE

. . . THE SIMMELIAN corpus may be conveniently divided according to the three viewpoints Simmel mentioned for analyzing things human: the individual, the social, and the objective. Under objective culture are to be found his various contributions to ethics, epistemology, aesthetics, and metaphysics, comment on which lies beyond the scope of this sutdy. Under the viewpoint of individual personality are to be found his studies of a few historic personalities—Michelangelo, Goethe, Rembrandt are the main ones—and occasional statements which reveal a rough working theory of personality. His aim in the study of the great personalities is always to disclose the inner unity, the form or essence, the "formula of the destiny of his soul" which underlies the diverse contents and expressions of the subject's life.

Simmel's theory of personality, like most prepsychoanalytic conceptions, is restricted to the psychology of the ego. It is dominated by two images. One image represents the self as a unity born of the interaction of psychic elements, just as the forms which sociology studies are unities born of the interaction among social elements. The other image, more specific and more often employed, presents the personality as divided into a central core and a periphery:

> In the inevitably symbolic language of all psychology: our soul seems to live in two layers, one of which is deeper, hard or impossible to move,

From Donald N. Levine, "Simmel and Parsons: Two Approaches to the Study of Society," a doctoral dissertation presented at the University of Chicago, 1957. Reprinted by permission of the author.

carrying the real sense or substance of our life, while the other is composed of momentary impulses and isolated irritabilities.[1]

We can designate certain relations of the ego to its contents only by the graphic symbol of a definite or a changing distance between them. . . . We divide our inner existence into a central ego and contents distributed around it.[2]

The more heterogeneous the peripheral contents, the more vividly does the form of the inner unity appear:

Conflicting tendencies can arise just because the individual has a core of inner unity. The ego can become more clearly conscious of this unity the more he is confronted with the task of reconciling within himself a diversity of group interests.[3]

Only the frequent alternation of [peripheral] contents reveals the ego to consciousness as the abiding center amidst the stream of psychic phenomena.[4]

Some of the other questions concerning the personality which Simmel discusses include: whether the individual is attracted more by others who are like him or unlike him, whether the ego is strong or weak, [and] whether [it is] more homogeneous or more differentiated.[5]

The forms of social interaction, comprising the third area of Simmel's contribution, may be arranged under these headings: *social processes, social types,* and *developmental* patterns. The following lists of these forms give but a crude picture of Simmel's sociological problems. Many of the terms involved have meanings that become clear only in context, and the mere titles of the problems

[1] Georg Simmel, *Soziologie* (Leipzig: Duncker und Humblot, 1908), p. 242. Kurt H. Wolff (ed.), *The Sociology of Georg Simmel* (New York: The Free Press of Glencoe, Inc., 1950), p. 300.

[2] Georg Simmel, *Die Philosophie des Geldes* (Leipzig: Duncker und Humblot, 1900), p. 536.

[3] *Soziologie, op. cit.,* p. 414. Georg Simmel, *Conflict and The Web of Group Affiliations,* translated by Reinhard Bendix and Kurt H. Wolff (New York: The Free Press of Glencoe, Inc., 1955), p. 142.

[4] *Soziologie, op. cit.,* p. 761.

[5] Many incisive propositions on ego psychology appear scattered over Simmel's work. Cf. Wolff, *op. cit.,* pp. 137, 217, 230, and 326; *Conflict . . . , op. cit.,* pp. 38, 49, 122, 153; *Die Philosophie des Geldes, op. cit.,* p. 529.

convey little idea of what particular questions are being discussed. . . .

*Social processes* refers to relatively simple, relatively stable, configurations of social interaction. The main social processes treated by Simmel are:

From *Über sociale Differenzierung:*

Attribution of guilt to a collectivity;
Group cohesion and solidarity (as a function of size and relations with outsiders);
Elementary collective behavior (the "social level");
Formation of parties, partisanship;
The division of labor.

From *Philosophie des Geldes:*

The forms of change of possessions (robbery, giving presents, reciprocal giving, tradition-sanctioned "gifts" and exchanges, haggling, exchange at fixed prices);
Money;
Representation;
The form of the double relationship whereby two phenomena which spring from the same *Grundmotiv* tend on the one hand toward reciprocal increase and, on the other, toward repression of one by the other;
The concentration of energy;
The forms of a fully rationalized order;
Personal independence in interpersonal relations;
Participation in associations that does not involve the whole personality;
The mutual reduction of both parties in a relation to the status of pure means;
Intensity of opposition between parties when they have a common origin.

From *Soziologie:*

Formal characteristics of the small group;
Forms of small groups (socialistic communities, religious sects, aristocracies);
The mass;
Relations of the individual to the norms of a group (custom, law, honor, individual morality);

*36680*

Number as a basis for group organization;
The social party;
Isolation;
Freedom, in the form of liberation from ties, power over others;
The dyad;
Monogamous marriage;
Associations of three or more members;
Reconciliation through a mediator;
*Divide et impera;*
Subordination under a single leader;
Opposition to the ruler;
Appeal to a higher tribunal;
Unification through common subordination (leveling, gradation);
Upward gradation;
Simultaneous super[ordination] and subordination;
Subordination of group to a member versus to an outsider;
Subordination under a plurality, where the plurality is [*a*] unified, [*b*] disunited, [*c*] stratified;
Subordination under ideal norms;
Forms of individual subordination to a group (social pressures, internalized social norms, objective morality);
The ruler's subjection of self to law he has himself made;
The contract;
Freedom of a small group within a large group;
Assimilation of the upward mobile section of an oppressed group to the ranks of the superordinate group;
Conflict;
Unification;
Hatred of the "enemy of the group";
Jealousy;
Envy;
Begrudging;
Competition;
Rivalry;
Unification through conflict;
Forms of termination of conflict (disappearance of the object of conflict, victory, compromise, conciliation);
Irreconcilability;
Confidence;
Acquaintance;
Discretion;

The secret;
Adornment;
The secret society;
The letter;
The confederation of associations;
Co-optation;
The hereditary office;
The facilitation or obstruction of entry or exit of members in a group;
Honor;
The group organ;
General forms of group persistence (rigidity and conservatism, flexibility and liberality);
Faithfulness;
Gratitude;
The boundary;
The fixed location as a center of activity;
The rendezvous;
The minority group;
Wandering;
Correlative formal categories applicable to any processes (the primary individual element, the narrow circle, and the wide circle).

From *Philosophische Kultur:*

Fashion;
Coquetry;
Love;
Play forms of association;
Sociability;
Social games;
Conversation.

If, instead of regarding association from the point of view of the total interactive process, one focuses on the typical characteristics of a person when engaging in the various sorts of interaction, one obtains a picture of particular social types. Besides discussing competition, for example, one may speak of *the competitor;* one may discuss *the coquette* as well as *coquetry.* [One] perspective discloses the invariant structures of social experience; the [other] reveals the variety of forms assumed by human nature qua social.

Simmel moves readily from the one sort of discussion to the

other. In many instances he finds it more useful to describe forms
of interaction from the vantage point of social type. Indeed, in
some cases this is necessary, for sometimes "characteristics of an
element which could originate only in the relation between this
and another element . . . come to be essential qualities of that
element, independent of all interaction." [6]

The main social types Simmel discusses are:

From *Philosophie des Geldes:*

The less involved party in a relation;
Forms determined by the individual's relation to money (the coveter of
money, the miser, the dissipator, the ascetic poor, the modern cynic,
the blasé type).

From *Soziologie:*

The mediator;
The nonpartisan;
The arbitrator;
The *tertius gaudens* (passive—enjoying advantages accidentally bestowed
by one of the conflicting parties; active—exploiting extant paralysis of
forces, or throwing his strength to one side);
The superordinate;
The subordinate;
The renegade;
The middleman;
The priest;
The merchant;
The woman;
The poor;
The bourgeois;
The stranger;
The aristocrat.

From *Philosophische Kultur:*

The adventurer;
The hero of fashion;
The feminine;
The masculine;
The forms of youth and age;

---

[6] *Soziologie, op. cit.,* p. 214.

The genius;
The coquette;
The professionals with little specialization but relatively high status (the lawyer, the salesman, the housewife).

By *developmental patterns* I refer to the more complex, diachronic forms which Simmel treats frequently enough to justify a separate heading. These include:

From *Über sociale Differenzierung:*

The differential progress of related forms;
The emergence of groups of individuals with similar interests who come from dissimilar backgrounds;
Social differentiation and its consequences;
Similarity of forms in the first and last stages of any development;
The pattern: Group G splits into factions $g_1$ and $g_2$, which are able to reunite into G again by relegating their doctrinal differences to the realm of individual preference.

From *Philosophie des Geldes:*

The tendency to develop a distinction between form and content and then come to value the form;
Lengthening means-ends chains to attain what is close at hand;
The tendency for things public to become more public, things private to become more private;
The differentiation of a unified state of things into one part which bears characteristics of the original whole and other contrasting parts;
The differentiation of an "immediate unity" into separate elements, which are later unified in a more intellectual and comprehensive synthesis.

From *Soziologie:*

Two modes of seeking social progress: [a] abolishing extant forms, [b] improving within extant forms;
Development from a local to a functional basis of social organization;
Development of functional organization from being based on "external, mechanical" criteria to being governed by rational criteria;
Development from inherently meaningful patterns of behavior to those, intrinsically mechanical and meaningless, which attain meaning by being organized in behalf of some higher purpose;
As group size increases, features common to its members which serve to

fuse them into a social unit decrease, and demands regarding the behavior of its members come to be of a more prohibitive, rather than positive, nature;

Internal development, and a rhythm of peace and conflict, are essential to the persistence of a group;

Individuality of being and behavior among individuals increases in direct proportion to the expansion of the social group.

STRATEGIC PROBLEMS IN SIMMEL

The following problems were selected with an eye to securing questions which are prominent in Simmel's work and which represent relatively unfamiliar writings to the English-reading audience. They include fashion (recurrent social process), the aristocrat (social type), social differentiation (developmental pattern), and his overriding ideological consideration: freedom.

*Fashion.*[7] As he so often does, Simmel begins the essay on fashion by speculating about some aspect of life in general in order to establish a point from which he may run a line of thought more or less directly to his topic. This characteristic of Simmel's style has earned it the epithet of "an oblique approach." In this case, it is the dualistic condition of life with which he begins—a dualism that cannot be directly apprehended, but can only be felt in the individual contrasts that mark our existence.

A series of such individual contrasts is then reviewed, from the physiological needs for movement/rest through the metaphysical conceptions of pluralism/monism to the political contrast of individualism/socialism. The history of society is seen as an interplay

---

[7] "Die Philosophie der Mode," *Moderne Zeitfragen*, XI (Berlin: Pan Verlag, 1905). A translation appears in *American Journal of Sociology*, LXII (May 1957), 541-59. In seeking some discussion of a social process that would be typical of Simmel and strategic in his thinking, I thought at first of using the essay on conflict here. This essay is one of his major achievements in sociology and is important in his thought. It demonstrates his conception of society as reciprocity of action, of the importance of nearness and distance in human relations, of the structural significance of dualism; and it identifies a number of less abstract forms related to the general process of conflict. This essay, however, has been paraphrased in English by Spykman, translated in full by Wolff, and analyzed in detail by Coser. It seemed more useful to present material with which the American reader would be less familiar. The essay on fashion is an equally important and distinguished piece of writing.

between the opposed tendencies: [that] for the individual to fuse himself with the group [versus that] to place himself outside the group. Imitation is a process which serves the former tendency; individualization is a medium for the latter.

Fashion is a form which combines both imitation and individualization. Fashion satisfies the individual's need to be different by the variety of contents it successively adopts, and by marking the domain of a particular class. In this latter respect, fashion is similar to honor, another form which imparts a common character to the members of a particular group and at the same time distinguishes them from those who stand outside the group.

That this purely formal social motive underlies the phenomenon of fashion is shown by the fact that fashions are often adopted for no objective, aesthetic, or other purposeful grounds whatsoever. Judging from the repugnant things that are sometimes in vogue, it would seem as though fashion desired to exhibit its power by getting us to adopt the most atrocious things for its sake alone. That both imitation and differentiation are indispensable components of fashion is shown by the following cases. In isolated, homogeneous, primitive societies there is little interest in differentiation, and so no show of fashions. Similarly, fashion was not present among the Venetian nobles, who wore black in order not to draw attention to their small numbers, and so could express no need to differentiate themselves in public. On the other hand, it is said that there was no ruling fashion in male attire in Florence toward the end of the *trecento,* in that everyone adopted a style of his own. Fashion was not present because the disposition to fuse with the collectivity was absent.

The upper class, most eager of all strata to maintain its inner solidarity and at the same time to distinguish itself from all other strata, originates the new fashions. Upward-mobile persons find in fashion an ideal means for imitating and identifying with the upper class. When a fashion is adopted outside the class that originates it, that class develops new fashions. This process repeats itself *within* the strata of the upper class. With the lowering of class barriers and the increase of wealth in a population, the process becomes progressively more frantic.

The dude is the leader of style—who is led by the new vogue.

The enemy of fashion represents the same form, under a negative sign. The fashionable individual derives the satisfaction of knowing that he represents something special and striking, while he feels inwardly supported by a set of persons who are striving for the same thing. He is envied as an individual, approved of as a member of a group. Fashion is thus an ideal field for individuals who are dependent, yet who demand a certain prominence.

As any vogue becomes widely accepted within a collectivity, it begins to die out as a fashion. Much of the charm of fashion is owing to this character of being at once novel and transitory, of being a "boundary" between being and not-being. At its apex, a fashion imparts a peculiarly strong sense of the present, an emphasis which also accentuates the sensation of change. Another reason for the hold of fashion on the modern mind is that the great, permanent, unquestionable convictions are continually losing strength, with the result that the transitory elements of life acquire more room for their activity. Fashion has thus gained increasing influence over taste, over theoretical convictions, even over the moral foundations of life.

Women are generally the staunchest adherents of fashion, for it provides a medium by which they can attain a certain individuation otherwise denied by their normally suppressed condition, and a status denied them by not having a calling or profession.

There are other needs which the form of fashion is especially suited to satisfy. Because its place in the individual is at the periphery of personality, it serves as a mask for refined and singular persons. Blind obedience to the standards of the general public becomes for them a means of reserving to themselves all manifestations of their feelings and tastes. Again, weak and retiring natures, vulnerable to mortification or shame at any exposure of themselves, seize on fashion as a kind of collective behavior in which feelings of shame have no place. Finally, because fashion affects only the externals of life, it gives the individual an easy way to express his solidarity with his time and society, and thereby enables him to devote the freedom given one in life to inner, more essential matters.

Fashion as an interpersonal phenomenon has a certain parallel within the personality. Tendencies both toward equalizing unification and individual demarcation can be found within an individual when he creates a personal style, a mode of conduct for himself which shows the pattern—rise, sway, and decline—of social fashion. One might say that personal fashion forms a limiting case of social fashion. Between the two phenomena is the case where pet terms are applied indiscriminately to all the objects within one's purview, usually by the members of a narrow circle. By so subjecting everything under a certain category, people gain a feeling of power—a feeling whose superficiality is betrayed by the rapidity with which such expressions pass by.

The total rhythm in which individuals and groups move has an important bearing on their relation to fashion. The lower classes are generally hard to move and slow to develop, while the upper classes are consciously conservative, often archaistic. Neither offers fertile ground for the vicissitudes of fashion. Fashion is, rather, the province of the middle classes, with their variable and restless rhythms. For this reason, the ascendance of the *tiers état* diffused and innervated the process of fashion; but this was also because frequent changes of fashion, implying as they do a huge subjugation of the individual, are a necessary complement of social and political freedom: "Man requires an ephemeral tyrant as soon as he has rid himself of the permanent and absolute one." [8]

Despite the transiency of particular fashions, the fashionable objects of the moment seem to promise a certain permanency. This is because fashion itself, as a social form, is immortal; some fashion or other is always with us. This becomes more than symbolic in the many instances when items once fashionable have been restored to fashion after lying forgotten for a while.

Although the power of fashion is great, it cannot exploit all objects with equal success. Some things are likely to become fashionable, just as some natural objects lend themselves readily to becoming material for art; others offer resistance. Everything "classical" is relatively far removed from fashion and alien to its spirit. By contrast, everything baroque and extreme seems to be drawn to fashion. Though fashion as a form is natural to man, the utterly unnatural fares well in the form of fashion.

*The aristocrat.* The problem of the nature of aristocracy not only

[8] *Ibid.,* p. 34.

indicates the sort of thing Simmel has to say about a social type, it also represents a theme recurrent in his thinking. Like few sociologists, . . . Simmel expresses great interest in differences of quality among people and experiences. He often speaks about *finer natures, more sensitive individuals, decisive personalities.* Such interest in the human elite is not unrelated to an interest in the social elite. In the "Exkurs über den Adel," [9] Simmel seeks to define the formal position of the latter, particularly as found in monarchies.

The form of the aristocracy depends in the first instance on its character as an intermediate structure (*Zwischengebilde*). This is so in two senses: horizontally, it is midway between the individual and the widest social circle; vertically, it is midway between the ruling power and the broad mass of political and social groups. It differs from the bourgeoisie, which it resembles in these respects, by being closed above and below. Entry into the ranks of the nobility is typically difficult. Departure from those ranks is, likewise, not easy but—once it is called for—it is complete and absolute. This sharp social demarcation of the aristocracy is reflected in two stipulations: the aristocrat may do what others may not, and he may not do things which are permitted to others.

It is clear that this formal character follows from the conditions of interaction in aristocracies. The same structure appears in the greatest variety of groups—in ancient Rome, under the Normans, in the *ancien régime,* and in the "aristocracies" of such smaller collectivities as labor groups, large family circles, and the clergy. This homogeneity of formal-sociological position is highlighted by the tendency of members of aristocracies of different lands to intermarry, in spite of the traditional localism of aristocratic groups; and by instances when connections among the nobility have provided some sort of community in nations otherwise unconsolidated.

Carrying the analysis further, we find that the sociological form distinctive of aristocracies derives from a unique relation between the general social content of the group and the individual existence of its members. Each member of an aristocracy participates in and avails himself of whatever is most valuable in all the members of the group. It is as though a substance of lasting value runs through

---

[9] *Soziologie, op. cit.,* pp. 732-46.

the blood of the various members of an aristocracy, generation after generation. Aristocracies have historically been in opposition to political centralization as representing a principle opposed to their own hereditary basis. Where access to high honors on a hereditary basis is proscribed, as in Russia before Czar Feodor, the formation of an aristocratic class is prevented. To assure the continuity of their "valuable substance," equality of birth is insisted on in marriage. This in turn confirms that closed-off, self-contained character of aristocracies which, above and beyond the cultivated bodies and manners of their members, is responsible for much of the aesthetic attraction which aristocracies have always exerted.

The importance of the family tree for aristocracy lies in its indication that the substance which forms the individual concerned is indeed the same substance which has passed through the whole line of noble stock. This preoccupation with maintaining oneself intact may explain the aristocrat's aversion toward work, which, after all, demands a submergence of the self in behalf of an object. Characteristic aristocratic activities, such as war and hunting, involve the predominance of the subjective factor. The work of the artist, which seeks to articulate the inner motion of a subject, bears the closest analogy to aristocratic activity; but it is an individuality, not a common substance handed down by family and class, which comes to expression.

The motive of superiority and social exclusiveness inclines aristocratic groups toward the use of secrecy, a device for heightening the wall against outsiders. At the political level, one notes that secrecy has always been among the requisites of political aristocracies—just as, conversely, the democratic principle is associated with the principle of publicity. Acting as an individual, however, the aristocratic personality despises concealment, because his inner certainty renders him indifferent to the regard of others.

The most crucial thing about aristocracy, however, is that the whole constellation of accumulated and traditional values which confront the noble-born does not have an objective, superindividual significance. These values come to their own, rather, only in the self-reliant, self-contained existence of individual aristocrats. Aristocracy thus represents a peculiar synthesis of two extreme conditions—when the individual is swallowed up by his group, and when

he stands, independent, in opposition to it. The weight of tradition the aristocrat must bear calls for strength and independence,
as well as responsibility. When the personalities involved are too
weak, the mere execution of traditional forms results in decadence.
In sum:

> By strictness of the aristocratic style of life, which creates the widest area
> of contact among its members; by the demand of equal rank in marriage,
> which effects a physiological guarantee of the qualitative and historical
> unity of the class; by the technique of its tradition, which accumulates
> the values and achievements of the family and class without loss—by
> these sociological means the aristocracy fuses its members to an other-
> wise unattainable degree into the collectivity. But this superindividual
> formation, so created, finds (more than any other collective structure) its
> meaning and purpose in the existence of individuals, in their might and
> meaning, in the freedom and self-sufficiency of their lives.[10]

*Social differentiation.* Differentiation as a state of social organization, as the division of labor in any of its forms, has—like conflict
or fashion—the status of a recurrent process. Viewed diachronically,
however, as the emergence of a more differentiated condition from
a more homogeneous and unified one, it refers to a developmental
pattern. In this sense, social differentiation constitutes the dominant
developmental pattern in Simmel's thought (as well as perhaps the
most prominent theme in the literature of social science).

At the most abstract level, Simmel is fond of showing how some
commonly accepted dualism has emerged from an originally undifferentiated state (*Indifferenzzustand*). Cognition, for example, begins in children and among primitive peoples purely as awareness
of impressions and ideas. The differentiation into a knowing subject and a known object comes about as a later development from
this original unity. Similarly, in the realm of volition, the distinction between a desiring subject and a valued object follows, logically and psychologically, the unitary experience of pure enjoying.

There are two main contexts in which Simmel applies this sort
of analysis to society. They appear in the two chapters, "Die Aus-
dehnung der Gruppe und die Ausbildung der Individualität," and
"Über die Kreuzung socialer Kreise," which he included both in

---

[10] *Ibid.*, p. 746.

*Über sociale Differenzierung* and in *Soziologie*. The central proposition of the former essay is that as the size of a group increases, its members become more unlike one another. The latter essay traces much the same pattern from a different viewpoint: the movement from propinquity to interest as a basis for association. The one chapter treats the small homogeneous group as an *Indifferenzzustand* from which the large group and differentiated individuals have emerged. The other chapter stresses the fusion of individual and group when kinship and locale are the principles of social organization, and how this condition becomes differentiated into a condition wherein individuals participate in a variety of more specific associations with only certain parts of their personalities. These two aspects of social differentiation are treated as separate developmental patterns; Simmel nowhere combines them in a single systematic analysis.

The correlation of individual differentiation with sociological expansion appears in the most diverse contents of social life. The powerful extended family is replaced by wider political groupings on the one hand, by individuals and their nuclear families on the other. Corporate guilt and the blood feud are succeeded by justice in the name of the larger society and individual responsibility. Unspecialized production for small markets gives way to production for large markets by means of considerable specialization on the part of producers.

The narrower group constitutes a sort of mean between the expanded group and individuality, i.e., these latter categories offer the same formal possibilities of social life that are combined in the first. A balance between individual and social tendencies is maintained in either case. The narrower the group, the less individuality its members have, but the more distinct the group itself is; in larger groups, the individuals have more room to differentiate themselves, but the groups as wholes tend to resemble one another. Individual uniqueness is attained at the cost of social uniqueness.

This correlation (which obtains synchronically, and in alternation, as well as in linear developmental patterns) is illustrated in antebellum American political life. The New England states were composed of small townships which absorbed and regulated much of the individual's life. The southern states, on the other hand,

were populated mostly by adventurous individuals with no inclina-
tion for local self-government. They formed large, colorless coun-
ties as administrative units, and their real political unity lay in the
state. The independent, almost anarchistic temperament of the
southerners was complemented by this abstract (state) political
structure, while the more strictly controlled citizens of New England created strongly individualized and autonomous local communities.

The realms of custom, law, and morality are seen as appropriate,
respectively, to the narrower group, the larger group, and the individual. Honor, formally similar to custom, is the technique of
control par excellence for the small group.

Simmel's chapter on "Die Kreuzung socialer Kreise" sees the development of human relations as analogous to the development of
thought. To the primitive mind, any coexistence of objects in time
and space is enough to bring about an association between the ideas
of these objects. For our conception of an object to free itself from
associations with attributes that are only accidental to it, we must
become aware of it in many different connections. In this way irrelevant associations get displaced by associations based on the content of what is perceived.

Similarly, in society individuals at first associate with whoever
moves in their immediate environment, without regard to one another's particular attributes. As society develops, individuals come
to establish contacts with persons outside these primary groups who
are related to them by actual similarity of talents, interests, and
activities. Just as a general concept binds together what a number
of different perceptual complexes have in common, so do practical
considerations bind together like-minded individuals who stem from
quite alien groups.

This pattern is illustrated in the early history of universities:
from unions of nationals to organization by faculties. Similarly,
English trade unions tended at first toward purely local organization, which was later replaced by a uniform organization of trades
on a nationwide basis. An intermediate stage in this transition is
represented by medieval group formation, in which the individual
came to have affiliations beyond those of his local community.
These were reached not through the individual but through the

corporate group—gild, monastery, or town. The modern situation in which the individual himself chooses from a vast number of associations on the basis of his various interests results in a more complex social structure, more differentiated and hence more determinate personalities, and greater social freedom.

*Freedom.* If one may speak about a dominant *Problematik* in Simmel's social thought, it would surely be the complex of questions dealing with individualism and freedom. Extensive discussions of these matters appear in each of his four sociological books. The crowning achievement of his life work was to have been a comprehensive treatment of the concept of freedom, including an interpretation of the significance of this concept for the actuality and the understanding of historical life. One can but deeply regret that a scant thirty pages of notes are all that were completed at the time of his death.[11]

Of the many aspects or kinds of freedom which Simmel mentions, three are of special sociological relevance. There is freedom in the sense of liberation from ties to things and others; freedom in the sense of the development of personality exclusively according to the laws of one's nature; and freedom in the sense of power to express one's will. Because the adoption of a money economy increases freedom in all three senses, Simmel devotes one sixth of *Philosophie des Geldes* to a study of the relations between money and freedom.

Widespread enjoyment of freedom in the first sense results above all from the numerical expansion of the group. . . . The small group is narrow in its restrictive control of the individual as well as in numbers. Expansion of the circles of social relationship increasingly frees the individual from the guardianship of community and church, from the demands of class and economic groups. Liberation from such connections is the great ideal of eighteenth century individualism.

Money advances this ideal in a number of ways. By providing a means whereby economic values can be condensed and mobilized, money extends the effective range of economic intercourse—and larger markets are larger circles. As a possession, money frees the individual from the responsibilities which usually attend possession

---

[11] "Über Freiheit: Bruchstücke aus dem Nachlass von Georg Simmel," *Logos,* XI (1922-23), 1-30.

of less mobile objects. Furthermore, money frees the subordinate from extensive duty to his lord by permitting him to discharge his obligations by handing over an object which may be acquired in any way he chooses: "Personal freedom can grow no greater, before the abolition of all rights of the landowner over subordinates, than when the obligation of the latter is turned into a money payment which the lord *must* accept." [12] Finally, as the perfect medium for impersonal relations among people, money helps to create a situation in which the individual is dependent on a host of other people for their services, but free and independent of them as particular persons. Any extension of objectivity in social life involves a corresponding increase in individuality.

Freedom as the unhampered development of personality according to one's nature is especially favored by the development of organization on a basis of interest rather than on the basis of propinquity. In a society that contains a large number of "interest" groups, the individual may find a collectivity within which to realize each of his several aspirations and at the same time enjoy the advantages of group membership. Despite the amount of association this implies, his individuality is assured by virtue of the unique constellation of groups to which he belongs. This idea of individualism—that the individual should realize what is unique in himself and thereby distinguish himself from all others—is that expressed in the nineteenth century, in theory by the Romantic Movement, in practice by the division of labor.

This situation is encouraged by money, for money promotes the formation of groups on a purely purposeful basis. But money furthers differentiation within the individual directly, not only as a by-product of differentiation in society. It does this by providing an effective means for distinguishing between the subjective center and the objective achievement of a person. The individual's performance may be paid for, while his person remains outside the transaction; or else the person as such may be supported (by contributions from many individuals), while his specific performances remain free from financial considerations. Freedom to live according to one's nature is advanced as the different qualities and powers of an individual unfold autonomously.

[12] *Philosophie des Geldes, op. cit.,* p. 301.

Money also plays an important role in increasing freedom in the sense of extending the individual's power over things. Of all objects, money offers the least resistance to an agent. It is the most "possessible" of all things, and hence completely submissive to the will of an ego. It can be come by in countless ways. Its possession can be indefinitely increased. Its uses are without number.

The increase of freedom is not the only direction taken by social developments, however, nor is freedom the only value to be realized in society. Human beings require a certain balance of freedom and constraint in order to live well. Just as, for example, the widespread diffusion of secret societies usually indicates a condition of regimentation and political oppression, i.e., it is a reaction stemming from the need for freedom; so, conversely, does ritual regulation within secret societies reflect their relative freedom from the larger society, i.e., it provides a condition in which human nature is kept in equilibrium through the establishment of norms that counterpart the norms of the larger society which have been rejected.

# THREE

# SIMMEL'S METHOD

### RUDOLF HEBERLE

. . . SIMMEL ACTUALLY intended more than a mere systematization of social forms. He made it clear enough that the conceptual distinction between *form* and *content* of society was "really nothing but an analogy," that both are "in reality inseparable elements of any social existence and process." [1] In his sociological papers he refers repeatedly to the "meaning" of social forms. The two questions—"What do the individuals mean by behaving in a certain way?" and "What is the objective meaning of the described action patterns in their lives?"—are constantly suggested, if not expressly put, to the reader.

As already pointed out, the search for the objective meaning leads beyond sociology, in the strict sense, into metaphysical interpretation. The inquiry into the subjective meaning requires the application of psychological knowledge and methods; yet, in its final intention, it does not aim at the regularities (laws) of psychic processes in the individual but at the causal understanding of the social-interaction patterns by which individuals are united into groups.

The objects of sociology are psychic processes which can be conceived by psychological categories. These are indispensable for the description of the facts, but they do not enter into the sociological intention which aims at the association process as such—like the

From Harry Elmer Barnes (ed.), *An Introduction to the History of Sociology* (Chicago: The University of Chicago Press, 1948). (Originally entitled "The Sociology of Georg Simmel.") Copyright 1948 by The University of Chicago. Reprinted by permission of the publishers.

[1] Georg Simmel, *Soziologie* (Leipzig: Duncker und Humblot, 1908), pp. 4, 5; also p. 10.

intention of a drama, which, although it can be understood only psychologically, is not directed at psychological insights but at those syntheses which the psychic processes form under the points of view of the tragic or of style or symbols of life.[2]

The problems of social psychology are, according to Simmel, merely special problems of individual psychology. Therefore, these arguments also apply to the objection that Simmel's sociology is not clearly distinguished from social psychology.

The nonpsychological character of Simmel's pure sociology can be exemplified by the principle of correlation between individuality and the expansion of the social circle. The principle, as such, does not contain any psychological theorem; it merely states an observable relationship between two elements of group structure.

Here, however, one weakness of Simmel's approach is revealed. Some of the phenomena could be made intelligible, even as evidence of structural principles, only by careful inquiry into psychic attitudes and processes. Simmel, instead, merely applies a rather general psychological hypothesis as "heuristic principle." The result is often mere conjecture rather than a real insight and secure knowledge. Furthermore, one can scarcely escape the impression that Simmel views society as an interplay of structural factors, in which the human beings appear as passive objects rather than as live and willing actors. Frequently, he refers to the inherent regularities of form principles as if these were the real moving forces in social life. Nowhere do we find a systematic analysis of the will-currents, the antagonisms and harmonies of interest and will which determine the course of individual and collective action and on which the very existence of associations depends.

However, the precise determination of the nature of social forms and the skillful application of the idea in Simmel's essays have opened a new angle of perception—a new outlook on social phenomena—which proves very fruitful in the analysis of concrete social situations, if applied with the necessary discretion. Simmel's procedure of staking off a field of investigation by abstracting a certain aspect (the "form" of social interaction) from the chaos of experienced reality is not unique, not peculiar to sociology; rather, it is the principle on which *all* specialization of the actual sciences

[2] *Ibid.*, pp. 17-19; cf. also the "Exkurs über Sozialpsychologie," *ibid.*, pp. 421-25.

has developed.[3] Simmel applied this principle to a field (sociology) in which, hitherto, the notion had prevailed that its specific object of cognition was not a new abstraction but, rather, a synthesis of the insights into social life gained by the existing specialized social sciences.

Among the critical objections to this idea of pure sociology, those offered by Hans Freyer deserve special attention because they raise a question of fundamental importance. Freyer points out that the conception of pure sociology as a sort of geometry of social phenomena may prove fatal, since it leads sociological thought off on a wrong track; phenomena that ought to be conceived as historical processes, imbedded in the context of the more or less unique situation in the flow of time, become fixed as static structures. Simmel, according to Freyer's criticism, tried to establish sociology as a *Logos-Wissenschaft*, which Freyer believes to be foreign to the very nature of its subject. Freyer, however, emphasizes the fact that, in spite of this fundamental error, Simmel's essays contain "excellent sociology," because, with a fine scientific tact, Simmel applied his approach only to such subjects as lend themselves to this kind of treatment, since they are, indeed, "timeless." [4]

The formal, or, as one might better say, the structural or morphological approach, applied even to the apparently most fluid social unions or groupings, is so widely different from the layman's point of view that it becomes immensely stimulating and challeng-

[3] Teaching disciplines which are formed for practical purposes may combine several such "sciences," e.g., geography. The field taught in the departments of sociology is, of course, composed of bits from a great many sciences, more or less well integrated by relation to the subject proper of sociology: the types of groups and social processes. Where "theory" is in disrepute, syncretism and a lack of interior, epistemological, and methodological order will be the consequence. Where Simmel's concept of "formal" sociology is adhered to with pedantry, the teaching will very likely lack substance and relevance to the significant problems of contemporary society.

[4] Hans Freyer, *Soziologie als Wirklichkeitswissenschaft* (Leipzig and Berlin: B. G. Teubner, 1930), pp. 46 ff., and 56-57. The same may be said of the work of Simmel's followers, especially Leopold von Wiese, who has attempted to develop systems (or parts of systems) of formal sociology. As long as they deal with phenomena of *universal* significance, especially with simple processes and relations, the approach proves satisfactory. Where, however, complex structures of a historically determined nature like the modern state are subjected to the same treatment, the approach has to be modified, or the resulting insights are of little significance.

ing. The student who is habitually inclined to think in compartments or fixed "contentional" categories is suddenly forced to draw comparisons between phenomena that seem to be distant in time or space and unrelated in quality, focusing his attention on the strictly social, that is, interactional, aspects. This, in itself, would be valuable in a propaedeutical sense. In addition, this approach is carried out with a meticulous casuistry in analysis. Never is Simmel content with general notions of social types; always he insists on defining the specific situations in which the phenomenon arises; always he forms, from general concepts, specific type concepts of well-defined "cases" of the general phenomenon studied.[5] In this respect, he is perhaps surpassed among his contemporaries only by Max Weber. Among the generation of his followers, Max Graf zu Solms and Leopold von Wiese have carried on this work of classification of forms of social interaction.[6]

While this method would finally result in a fruitless play of the mind—and, in fact, this danger zone is often touched in Simmel's essays—Simmel succeeds in making it a meaningful endeavor. This is accomplished by the introduction to the "form" analysis, of psychological interpretations, often of a very subtle character. Spykman[7] points out that Simmel agreed that pure sociology alone cannot convey a full understanding of society, that it needs supplementing by psychological and "factual" inquiries. As an illustration we may note his observation that conflicts between individuals intimately related by kinship or other close personal ties tend to be more bitter than those between comparatively strange and loosely

[5] Compare Simmel's own statement (*Soziologie, op. cit.*, p. 10): "Even an approximate dissolution of societal forms into simple elements [as in geometry] cannot be hoped for in the near future. Consequently, sociological forms if they are to be to some degree definite can be valid only for a relatively small range of phenomena. If one says, for instance, that super- and subordination is a form found in almost any human society, little will be won with such general statement. What is necessary is the consideration of the various ways of super- and subordination, of the special forms of their realization. These will lose in universality of validity the more concretely they are defined."

[6] Max Graf zu Solms, *Bau und Gliederung der Menschengruppen*, I. Teil (Karlsruhe: 1929); and *Führerbestellung: Bau und Gliederung der Menschengruppen*, II. Teil (Leipzig: 1932); also L. von Wiese and H. Becker, *Systematic Sociology* (New York: John Wiley & Sons, Inc., 1932).

[7] Nicholas J. Spykman, *The Social Theory of Georg Simmel* (Chicago: The University of Chicago Press, 1925).

related individuals. This is in itself a rather common-sense observation. The real value of Simmel's analysis lies in the fine distinctions between various typical constellations and in the sociopsychological explanations or interpretations.[8] The same manifestations of conflict may be due to a wide variation of motivations and may, therefore, be of quite different meaning for the life of the social groups in which they occur. Furthermore, violent conflicts, such as occur in intimate relations (e.g., in marriage), just because of a profound community of values among the partners, without endangering the relation as such, would definitely destroy any relation of less intimate character. Incidentally, these subtle differentiations of configurations (or forms) and motivations in social relations suggest the necessity of careful theoretical preparation and utmost caution in any quantitative inquiry into social attitudes and processes.

Simmel's interpretation of the trends of social change in contemporary Western society can hardly be said to be original. It is essentially a synthesis of the ideas developed previously by Marx, Tönnies, Durkheim, and others.

On the whole, his sociological interpretations, although extremely intelligent and subtle, do not betray a great deal of firsthand experience and contact with the great social movements and important societal events of his time. This may partly explain the lack of new original insights into the great social questions of the period.[9]

It seems that Simmel's interest in sociology originated not from an immediate concern with the social problems of contemporary society but, rather, from a philosophic endeavor to clarify its position in a system of sciences. Obviously, Simmel's occupation with problems of ethics and morals (Moralphilosophie) also led him into a discussion of norms and values in their relation to social life.

---

[8] Soziologie, op. cit., pp. 205-10.

[9] It seems symptomatic that Simmel's illustrations referring to the labor problem are almost exclusively taken not from German conditions but from the British Labor Movement or from the sphere of the domestic-servant problem, where Simmel had, of course, firsthand experiences. It is, furthermore, symptomatic that the rich sources of socioeconomic surveys, dissertations, and semi-official inquiries which had resulted from the influence of the historical school in economics in Germany have scarcely been utilized by Simmel, while he gives ample references to ancient and medieval history. The question of the sources of Simmel's knowledge of the social world can, of course, merely be stated, not answered, in the framework of this chapter.

These reservations have to be made in order to arrive at a fair appreciation of Simmel's work. Its real and lasting value lies not so much in the new knowledge of society it conveys as in the contribution to the classification of the purpose and procedure of sociology. Even his most severe critics acknowledge the significance of Simmel's idea of sociology as a systematic analysis of social forms: "The influence of Simmel's concepts of 'social form' is present in contemporary sociology, even where the idea of pure sociology in Simmel's sense is rejected." [10] It is Simmel's method and procedure of analysis rather than the content of his findings which constitute his unique and lasting contribution to the advancement of sociology. Thus we are confronted with the paradox that the philosopher who started out to redefine the subject matter of sociology gained his place among sociologists rather because of his methodological ideas. . . .

[10] Freyer, *op. cit.*, p. 47. The influence of Simmel's ideas on American sociology cannot be traced within the limits of this chapter.

# FOUR

# THEORY AND TRAGEDY
# OF CULTURE

### RUDOLPH H. WEINGARTNER

. . . HUMAN BEINGS necessarily transcend the processes of their own lives. Everywhere the process of experience becomes objectified: life brings forth numerous worlds of objects which, following ordinary usage rather than Simmel's, we call *objects of culture*.[1] Works of art, religious dogmas and institutions, philosophical doctrines, propositions and systems of science, moral precepts and codes, laws and legal systems, and the like are all products of life which, having been created, have then gone on to maintain their own existence, free both from the lives that created them and from other lives, contemporaneous with and following those of their creators: "To analyze the construction of this multiplicity of worlds and their special structures is the task of the philosophy of culture."[2] In fulfilling this function, the philosopher is "epistemologist";[3] he determines the character of the forms which give shape to the various worlds and the content to which shape is given. Less

From Rudolph H. Weingartner, *Experience and Culture* (Middletown, Conn.: Wesleyan University Press, 1962). Copyright © 1960, 1962, by Rudolph Herbert Weingartner. Reprinted by permission of Wesleyan University Press.

[1] Simmel's more specific conception of culture will be discussed in the pages which follow.

[2] Max Nobs, *Der Einheitsgedanke in der Philosophie Georg Simmels* (Bern: Haupt, 1926), p. 53.

[3] *Epistomology* is here understood in an extended sense: it pertains to the analysis of *all* forms, their logic and their function in experience, and not only to cognition. It comes to include much of Simmel's conception of philosophy of culture. For this, Simmel's broadened meaning of the term, see *Die Probleme der Geschichtsphilosophie* 4th ed. (München und Leipzig: Duncker und Humblot, 1922), pp. 197-98, note 1.

narrowly, he subjects the different modes of experience to analysis. . . .

The starting point for this investigation will be Simmel's own conception of culture which makes central neither the objects created by men, nor the process by which these objects are created, but the process of their reassimilation. Works of art or systems of science have their genesis in the experience of men. Because of this, their origin, and because of what they are, Simmel adopts Hegel's term and calls the totality of such human products *objective spirit*.[4] Men are surrounded by objective spirit, by the products of past and contemporary experience. Culture (or better, cultivation) designates a particular relation between the individual and objective spirit; it is a process whereby the individual interiorizes the objects he finds everywhere around him.[5]

Simmel makes use of an analogy in his effort to explicate his conception of culture: he begins by sketching the career of a fruit tree. Under the care of a gardener, a tree bearing wooden, sour, inedible fruit comes to bear the fruit that graces our table. The tree was found in a natural state and was cultivated. In one sense of "nature," the original tree, the process of transformation, and the final product are all natural. Nowhere was nature as the "all-encompassing complex of phenomena, bound together in causal sequences," [6] defied or counteracted. But in another sense of "nature," the natural condition of the tree was transformed into a cultured state: nature has given way to culture.

Not all changes constitute cultivation. Had the tree been fashioned into a mast of a schooner, the process of manufacture would not have been one of cultivation. The future state must be

. . . latent in the *natural structural relations or motive powers* of the subject. . . . The pear tree itself seems to us cultivated, because the gardener,

---

[4] For example, "Der Begriff und Tragödie der Kultur," in Gertrud Simmel (ed.), *Philosophie der Kunst* (Potsdam: Kiepenheuer, 1922), pp. 223, 224. (Hereafter referred to as "Begriff und Tragödie der Kultur.")

[5] Simmel's term is *culture* (*Kultur*), although, as can already be noted, he uses it to refer to the process which is usually indicated by the term *Bildung*. In English we shall make use of the term *cultivation* as well as *culture*.

[6] Georg Simmel, "Vom Wesen der Kultur," in Michael Landmann and Margarete Sussman (eds.), *Brücke und Tür: Essays des Philosophen zur Geschichte, Religion, Kunst und Gesellschaft* (Stuttgart: Köhler, 1957), p. 87. (Hereafter referred to as "Wesen der Kultur.")

after all, develops only those possibilities which rest in the organic predisposition of its natural form, bringing it to the most perfect unfolding of its own nature.[7]

And what is more, this unfolding requires the help of the gardener. If, without the aid of his skill, the fruit borne by a tree is delicious to the human palate, the tree cannot properly be called cultivated; it is in a natural state and its growth is only a natural process.

Given this account of the pear tree, three components that enter into Simmel's conception of culture may be isolated. First, culture is a process—cultivation. It is the transformation of an individual from one state to another, in some sense a higher, more perfect one. Second, the original state of the individual, the starting point of the process, is his natural state. Culture, then, is a kind of growth or development, an unfolding of an individual's potential. Finally, Simmel's understanding of culture requires that the transformation make use of objects which are external to the individual.

Although these components of culture go to make up Simmel's conception, they are not arbitrarily chosen. In the first place, Simmel would claim that he is making explicit what is contained in the usual meaning of the term. But second—and of far greater importance here—his conception of culture is closely related to his more general philosophic position, and only by being placed in that context will it become intelligible.

Life, understood as more-life, is a process, whether or not it is one of cultivation. Moreover, the starting point of life is inevitably that state in which the individual comes into the world. But when Simmel stipulates that the development called *cultivation* must be "in the direction of an inner, original nucleus, a perfecting of the being according to the norm, as it were, of its own significance, in the direction of its profoundest drives," he means to designate something more specific than the life process which each individual cannot help but live. The "natural structural relations or motive powers" [8] to which Simmel refers *may or may not* be actualized in the course of a lifetime. For there may be distortion as well as unfolding. There is present in every individual

---

[7] *Ibid.*, p. 87; italics in original. The nature of the potentiality here involved will be examined in a moment.

[8] *Ibid.*, pp. 88, 87, respectively.

. . . that into which the psyche can develop at all; [it] already lies in any given state as something that urges on; it is etched into the psyche as with invisible lines; despite the fact that in regard to its content it is often unclear and realized only fragmentarily, it still constitutes a positive directedness.[9]

Simmel uses expressions such as *structural relations* and *nucleus;* he speaks of a single core, a directedness, a pointing, and of an impulse in one direction. The various capacities of an individual are apparently so interconnected that they constitute a unity. Just this configuration of just these potentialities makes up a unique individual. It is this individuality which must unfold in cultivation.

There is a danger of misinterpretation. The unity or connectedness of an individual's capacities might be understood in such a way that, in effect, their multiplicity reduces to a single potentiality. Then, since the process of life must begin with and operate upon this single potentiality, it could not help but actualize it. All living would be growth in the same sense; all differences would be matters of degree. If, for the moment, we ignore the stipulation that external objects must be assimilated, this understanding of the relations among human capacities would lead us to the conclusion that all living is cultivation.

But an individual's capacities are not in this way unified. "The unity of the psyche [is] not a formal band, which always encloses in the same way the unfolding of its particulars." [10] It is etched into the individual with *invisible* lines; the unity of the personality is not a constricting force, but a balance or harmony of possibilities and powers. Rather than being ascertained as a fact, it is always apprehended as a goal to be pursued. For want of a better word, the "indefinable personal unity" [11] may be called a *dynamic* unity which cannot remain static as long as the individual lives.

Because life is a process, it necessarily involves some actualization of some capacities. Conversely, it would be absurd to imagine an individual becoming or doing something for which he did not possess the potentiality. However, not *any* development of potentialities constitutes the kind of growth which Simmel calls cultivation.

[9] *Ibid.,* p. 88.
[10] "Begriff und Tragödie der Kultur," *op. cit.,* p. 225.
[11] *Ibid.,* p. 225.

All sorts of knowledge, virtuosities, or refinements a man might have cannot yet determine us to attribute genuine culture to him, as long as these [modifications] operate only as additions which come to his personality from a realm of value that is and ultimately remains external to it. To be sure, in such a case a man is cultured, but he is not cultivated.[12]

When an individual develops only one aspect of the complex of capacities given him, when he pursues only one kind of activity and allows other abilities to wither, the state which undergoes transformation is not his "natural" one, just as the manufacture of a mast from the trunk of a tree is not based upon the "nature" of the tree. Neither the process of change nor the state which results can therefore be called *culture. Nature,* then, takes on a still more specific meaning; it designates more than whatever is native. Singly or together, all of an individual's abilities are natural. But the particular configuration of powers he possesses, the dynamic unity of all of his potentialities constitute *his* nature. The development of one capacity to the exclusion of others (whether it is the mathematical ability of a man or the structural strength of a tree trunk) is therefore not the development of the nature of the individual, but constitutes its distortion. Hence, in such a case the process is not one of cultivation.[13]

Because an individual's nature does not reduce to a single potentiality, cultivation allows and requires the development of different capacities to different degrees and at different times. Human abilities and interests constitute a "bundle of lines of growth which stretch out in quite different directions and to quite different lengths." [14] Their development, however, counts as cultivation only when each serves to develop the individual's personality as a unity. In a characteristically Simmelian formulation, "culture is the road from a closed unity through an unfolded multiplicity to an unfolded unity." [15]

Although Simmel is careful to point out that cultivation is by

[12] *Ibid.,* p. 226.

[13] A fruit tree, for Simmel, does not have *a* nature in this sense. The dynamic unity of different capacities apprehended as a goal to be pursued clearly requires consciousness. Accordingly, the analogy admittedly breaks down. See "Wesen der Kultur," *op. cit.,* pp. 88-89.

[14] "Begriff und Tragödie der Kultur," *op. cit.,* p. 225.

[15] *Ibid.,* p. 225.

no means the only activity of value,[16] it is not surprising that it is of great interest to him. Cultivation preserves and exploits the uniqueness of the individual. He who submerges himself completely in one or another objective order is in danger of never realizing his individuality. He becomes a scientist, artist, or philosopher and his particular personality, consisting of a particular balance among skills and capacities, remains unrealized. Simmel is concerned with cultivation, because to develop the personality as a whole is tantamount to giving a unified form to the process of life. Cultivation is, so to speak, the ethical aspect of *Lebensphilosophie,* for it means treating one's own life as an object that must be continuously shaped.

The first two components of Simmel's conception of culture, *transformation* and *nature,* have been explicated. Together they specify a certain type of growth. There remains the third ingredient, the use of objects that are external to the individual. The psyche can reach certain perfections of the personality "purely from inside . . . exclusively with its subjective personal powers." He has in mind "religious ecstasies, moral self-sacrifice, masterful intellectuality, harmony of collective life." None of these, however, is cultivation properly speaking, because cultivation requires that "man assimilates into his development something that is external to him; [it requires that] the path of the psyche go via values and sequences that are not themselves subjective and psychic." [17]

For Simmel's stipulation that cultivation must involve objects external to the individual, there are two reasons—though they are not of equal importance. Common speech understands cultivation to be a certain relationship between an individual and objective spirit: colloquially, to be cultured is to be versed in the arts and sciences. What is more important, however, is the fact that, aside from a few exceptions, human potentialities *are* capacities for activity in the various realms of objective spirit. Their development,

---

[16] *Ibid.,* pp. 226-27.

[17] *Ibid.,* pp. 226-27. Given Simmel's assumptions, one might quarrel with his view that there can be a purely subjective development of a personality. Strictly speaking, every experience contains an objective element, if only because experience *creates* objects. What does distinguish the examples here cited from those which Simmel wishes to call cultivation proper is that they make relatively little use of already existing objects and norms.

whether the individual *cultivates* his personality or whether he one-sidedly develops a *fraction* of his abilities, requires external objects as means.

Simmel's conception of culture may now be given its final formulation. Culture "signifies that kind of individual perfection which can be carried out only by means of an assimilation or utilization of a superpersonal structure that lies in some sense external to the subject." [18] In his posthumously published lectures on pedagogy, Simmel articulates this concept somewhat more fully. Since in these lectures Simmel was concerned with education in a narrower sense, we must therefore generalize from the cognitive realm to include all of objective spirit.

> Education is neither the mere *having* of the content of knowledge nor is it merely a contentless state of being of the psyche. Rather, he is educated whose objective knowledge has entered into the vitality of his subjective development and existence, and whose mental energy is filled with as large as possible and always growing area of contents that are valuable in themselves.[19]

Cultivation overcomes the subject-object distinction between the individual and objective spirit. The process bridges the gap between the individual who pursues his own career and the external objects which surround him. After all, the worlds of art, science, religion, philosophy, morality, and so on, do not consist of unformed contents, but of objects that have already been formed. And while we can treat existing works of art, and so on, merely as contents, that is, as materials to which *our* experience will now impart a form, this is to ignore the fact that they are already objects in virtue of previous experience. When we treat the components of objective spirit as no more than a sequence of contents, we fail to recognize its objectivity.

In principle we are capable of experiencing the components of objective spirit as objects, because they are themselves the products of experience, because they are the expressions of lives like our own. The form which makes them objects is not alien, because it is human. Thus, when the process of cultivation is successful, it

---

[18] *Ibid.*, p. 233.
[19] Georg Simmel, *Schulpädagogik*, Karl Hauter (ed.) (Osterwieck/Harz: Zickfeldt, 1922), p. 33; italics in original.

relates the individual to the objects which surround him; it makes him at home in the cosmos of human devising. By functioning in his development, the objects become the objects *of* the individual. They become *his* objects in that they are objects of his unified personality; they are integrated into the course of his life.

Because objective spirit was produced in human experience, it is in principle accessible to men. Nevertheless, there are difficulties. The objects I seek to assimilate in the cultivation of my own personality are the products of lives and times different from my own. They were not created to be culture-values, that is, to be means to my fulfillment.

> Operative in the founder of a religion, in the artist, in the statesman and inventor, in the scholar and in the legislator is . . . the discharge of the forces of their being, the mounting of their lives to that level on which they release the contents of cultural life. . . .[20]

The powers and natures of *other* men, living in *different* contexts, provided the impetus which produced the objects surrounding me. Objective spirit consists of the products of human experience; but the life which entered into them is not my life; their time is not my time.[21]

Moreover, the release of inner tensions is but the *terminus a quo* of the components of objective spirit. In the very same creators a second factor, the *terminus ad quem,* is also operative: "the passion for the thing, in the autonomous perfection of which the subject has become indifferent to itself and extinguished." [22] Objective spirit is the product of free activity; its objects were created as works of art, science, philosophy, religion, law, or whatever, and were shaped in accordance with the criteria of the applicable form. They were produced as, and now are, *objective values*—that is, objects whose value is determined by the norms of their form, having a place in the hierarchy of values generated by aesthetic, cognitive, philosophical, or legal principles of judgment. The *cultural value*

---

[20] "Begriff und Tragödie der Kultur," *op. cit.,* p. 235.
[21] The difficulty here indicated is aggravated whenever an object is not the product of a single life, but is the result of a process of production organized on the principle of division of labor. For a discussion of this problem, see particularly *ibid.,* pp. 243-44, 252.
[22] *Ibid.,* p. 235.

of a work of art or a scientific theory depends on what it does or is capable of doing for me; it depends on how susceptible it is to integration into the course of *my* life, on how "useful" it is in the development of my personality. Initially, a thing has objective value (for the principle by which it has value is that which makes it an object). Subsequently, it attains cultural value or indeed it may fail to do so. The objective and the cultural values of an object are therefore not identical.

It is not difficult to find examples of this disparity. Writing in the first decades of this century, Simmel observes that the art of antiquity has become relatively inaccessible. Objectively—that is, judged by aesthetic standards—the sculptures of Phidias are still among the greatest accomplishments of human art. But, given the life and temper of the pre-World War I period, their cultural value is relatively low. Men find it difficult to make use of these objects in the development of their own personality; the sculptures remain "external," alien to their lives. The history of science yields a quite different instance of this situation. Without a doubt, the development of physics in the latter part of the nineteenth century constituted immense progress, as judged by the norms of the scientific enterprise. It is equally clear, however, that the role which the later science can play in the growth of an individual—as a whole, not as scientist—is not what it had been.[23]

To understand the problems inherent in the process of cultivation, the realm of objective spirit must be subjected to further examination.

. . . The realm of cultural products grows and grows as if an inner logical necessity brought forth one component after another, frequently almost unrelated to the will and the personality of the producers and as if untouched by the question as to the number of subjects who

---

[23] The objective value need not be "higher" than the cultural value. It may happen (and it may be true of our time) that those objects which enter significantly into the lives of many individuals have little objective value. The art which is most widely enjoyed, the ideas and theories which have the greatest currency and the deepest effect may well be shabby and insignificant, when judged by the standards of art and philosophy. When this is the case, when the significant *cultural* values of a period are in this sense hollow and of no consequence, a state of cultural decadence is defined, a state which must reflect the emptiness of the lives of the individuals which make up society. See *ibid.*, p. 234.

assimilate this realm and are led to its cultural significance, and to what degree of profundity and completeness they assimilate it.[24]

First of all, the realm of objective spirit grows; it literally becomes larger and larger, so that it becomes increasingly impossible for an individual to assimilate the whole of it, to have all of it enter into his own development, to convert all of it into cultural value. The very fact of an ever-increasing number of potential cultural values in itself gives rise to feelings of alienation. It will not do to say that the individual may ignore whatever he cannot assimilate.

The store of objectified spirit which grows to the point of becoming incalculable makes demands of the subject, arouses velleities in him, chastises him with feelings of his own inadequacy and helplessness, weaves him into a total context whose totality he cannot evade, without, however, enabling him to master its particular contents. In this way the typical problematical situation of modern man comes into being: the feeling that he is surrounded by a legion of elements of culture which are not meaningless for him, but which, at bottom, are also not meaningful. Their bulk is depressing, because the subject cannot internally assimilate every detail; nor, however, can he simply reject it, since potentially, as it were, it belongs to the sphere of his cultural development.[25]

The process of cultivation is that by which the individual relates himself to the objective spirit. To the extent to which the sheer magnitude of objects prevents their mastery, complete cultivation has failed.

The realm of objective spirit is constantly enlarged; yet, in the process of cultivation, the problem of size is only a secondary one. The heart of the difficulty lies in the fact that "the contents of culture . . . follow a logic which is independent of their *cultural* purpose and leads further and further away from it." [26] There are, as Simmel once put it, not one, but two ways of being "consequent." [27] The first pertains to the logic of biography: a given

---

[24] *Ibid.*, p. 246.
[25] *Ibid.*, p. 250.
[26] *Ibid.*, p. 253; italics in original.
[27] *Schulpädagogik, op. cit.*, p. 56.

experience implies another, subsequent one, which leads to a further unfolding of the individual's personality. To be "consequent" in this sense is to follow the dictates of cultivation. The second sense is more familiar. Any given experience has a particular form. In virtue of that form, the experiencing subject enters an objective realm which is ruled by its own laws. If the given experience is followed by a subsequent one—this time according to the logic of the form—it is *objectively* "consequent." The two logics, the subjective one of cultivation and the objective one of the form, are independent of each other, while the individual's experience has its place in both. Given any particular experience, in other words, *two* "next" experiences which need not be the same are implied.

At this point it might be objected that this dual logic raises no special difficulty. As long as our concern is with cultivation, the individual is clearly called upon to be biographically "consequent"; he must simply ignore the demands of the logic of the form. But this escape does not exist for Simmel. Cultivation requires the assimilation of the components of objective spirit and hence demands that one does enter into its different forms. The cognitive, artistic, religious, philosophical enterprises each have their own laws and disciplines; one must follow these laws not only to contribute creatively to these worlds, but to understand and appreciate the objects that already exist. To succeed in developing its capacities, the self must make the objects of the different worlds *its* objects. But to be able to do so, the individual stands the risk of being drawn into that world and of having his goal of cultivation frustrated.

> By these contents which the self shapes in a particular way, the external worlds seize the self in order to draw it into themselves; in that these worlds form the contents according to *their* demands, they prevent the contents from being centered around the self.[28]

An analysis of Simmel's concept of culture shows that in the process of cultivation the individual is subjected to two different sets of demands which are completely independent of each other. The demands are not contradictory, for they *may* be the same. In-

[28] "Begriff und Tragödie der Kultur," *op. cit.*, p. 242; italics in original. Also see "Der Henkel," in *Philosophische Kultur*, 2nd ed. (Leipzig: Kröner, 1919), pp. 123-24 (translated in Kurt H. Wolff [ed.], *Georg Simmel, 1858-1918* [Columbus, Ohio: Ohio State University Press, 1959], pp. 274-75).

deed, it is the mark of the genius that for him the two roads, that of his own development and that of form, very frequently coincide.[29] The genius is seldom torn between the two ways of being "consequent": the same experience will tend to satisfy both claims. The genius, however, is the exception. Most men are faced with conflicting demands and fail to meet the challenge. Either they never come to develop their capacities or, like the fruit tree that becomes a mast, they are caught up in the logic of an objective world, with the result that their growth is distorted. The world which was to be the means to his development comes to claim the individual as its servant.

> It is the conception of all culture that the mind creates an independent object through which the development of the subject from itself to itself takes its path; but just in becoming objective, this integrating element, which is a condition of culture, is predetermined to its own development. It still uses up the powers of subjects, it still pulls subjects into its own orbit, yet without leading the subjects to their own highest level. The development of the subjects cannot take the same path as that of the objects; but when they nonetheless follow the development of the objects, the subject's development goes astray in a blind alley, or its innermost and most intimate life is emptied out.[30]

The conflict implicit in Simmel's conception of culture is a characteristically tragic one. As in a tragedy, "those destructive forces that are directed against a being" do not come to it from the outside, having nothing to do with his own nature and action. Rather, they originate "in the deepest layers of precisely that being itself." The destruction of the individual "fulfills a destiny which was planted in him and which is, so to speak, the logical development of just that structure by means of which that being has built up its own reality."[31] In the process of cultivation, the destructive power —the necessity of obedience to the logic of the forms—has the same origin as the constructive one: the assimilation of objective spirit, for the sake of the individual's growth. Everything that has cul-

---

[29] The theme of the genius is discussed in various places. For the best statement, see *Goethe*, 4th ed. (Leipzig: Klinkhardt & Biermann, 1921), Chap. 1, "Leben und Schaffen," pp. 1-19.

[30] "Begriff und Tragödie der Kultur," *op. cit.*, p. 249.

[31] *Ibid.*, p. 249.

tural value has objective value. If an object's cultural value is to be realized, it must be assimilated as an object.

At bottom, the conflicting demands which culture places upon the individual are symptomatic of the tension contained in Simmel's dual definition of life. Life is more-life—it is a process which pushes on, seeking to follow its own developmental laws. But life is also more-than-life; it is formative and produces objects that are independent of it. For life as process to continue, it requires the aid of form which, in its stability, is the antithesis of process. Hence, life as process stands the risk of being shattered on the surface of the very object it has produced.[32] To continue, it must both produce and overcome the components of objective spirit; it must both be formative and dissolve form. At the root of the conflict of culture

> . . . is the completely fundamental antithesis between the principle of life and the principle of form. Since life can only express itself in forms, this opposition manifests itself in every particular case as the struggle between the form just now discharged by life and that which it had formerly produced as its shape, its designatable quality, its language.[33]

[32] That Simmel's theory of culture and analysis of alienation resemble the dialectic of Marx's philosophy of history is not a coincidence. To begin with, both Marx and Simmel are students of Hegel's philosophy and derive from it important elements of their own doctrines. But more directly, Simmel was aware of the work of Marx. He finds no fault with Marx's position to the effect that the political and ideological superstructure of a society lags behind changes in the modes of production, finally leading to a "contradiction." For Simmel, Marx does not go far enough: there is tension between the life of the individual or society and *all* of the products created by men. The dialectic must be generalized. A second important difference between Marx's theory of the dialectic of history and Simmel's theory of culture is that the former might be called a cosmic comedy, the latter a human tragedy. In Marx's conception, the opposition between the economic order and all others will finally be resolved in the synthesis of the classless society. Simmel's is a *Lebensphilosophie:* the tension he is concerned with has its origin in the nature of human life and will exist as long as life exists. Of course, even if Simmel is granted his theory of culture, it is a second question as to whether it need be apprehended as a tragedy, that is, whether it justifies Simmel's *fin de siècle* pessimism with regard to the chances of the development of the human personality. For references to Marx, see: "Begriff und Tragödie der Kultur," *op. cit.,* p. 250; *Geschichtsphilosophie,* 4th ed. (München and Leipzig: Duncker und Humblot, 1922), pp. 207-27; *Philosophie des Geldes,* 4th ed. (München and Leipzig: Duncker und Humblot, 1922), pp. 456-79; "Wandel der Kulturformen," in *Brücke und Tür, op. cit.*

[33] *Lebensanschauung,* 2nd ed. (München and Leipzig: Duncker und Humblot, 1922), p. 157.

# FIVE

# MONEY AND ALIENATION

## ALBERT SALOMON

. . . SIMMEL's SOCIOLOGICAL interest was the result of Spencer's and of Marx's influences. Like Tönnies and the Webers, Simmel was fascinated by the work of Karl Marx. He was of the opinion that it was possible to preserve the scientific truth that was hidden in this political eschatology. Over and over again he remarked that his efforts were directed to finding a more profound and comprehensive basis of the dialectical materialism in the very structure of the life-world of human beings. Three times[1] he attacked this problem. He established the thesis that the very character of human existence is dialectical. According to Simmel, the unending continuity of the process of life clashes necessarily with the acts of individuation, with the creative acts in which the social institutions are established. These acts transcend the flux of life. Their achievements have a reality of their own, a being beyond the continuity of the stream of life. This is the inescapable destiny of man, his tragedy and the crisis of civilization. Simmel calls this dualism of life and the objects of the mind *the objectivation of the human mind*. Marx had called it *the self-alienation*. Simmel asserted that this dialectic is not a historical phenomenon of capitalism, but the general destiny of mature civilizations. In such situations the works of men lose the human coefficient and are established in autonomous contexts of

From Georges Gurvitch and Wilbert E. Moore (eds.), *Twentieth Century Sociology* (New York: The Philosophical Library, Inc., 1945). (Originally entitled "German Sociology.") Reprinted by permission of the publishers.

[1] Georg Simmel, "Der Begriff und die Tragödie der Kultur," in *Philosophische Kultur* (Leipzig: Kröner, 1919); *Der Konflikt der modernen Kultur* (Leipzig: Duncker und Humblot, 1918); "Die Krisis der Kultur," in *Der Krieg und die geistigen Entscheidungen* (Leipzig: Duncker und Humblot, 1917).

their own. These intermediate layers of civilization threaten the genuine and natural unity between man and his values. In particular, all mature civilizations face this problem. Men have created such a diversity of products and works that frequently means are considered to be ends. Simmel states that the confusion of the means-end relationship and the clash between the subject and the objects of the world are the very contents of the dialectics of human life. Man always is in danger of being slain by the objects of his own creation. This thesis of Simmel's is the humanization of Marx's objectivation of the consciousness and of the theory of self-alienation.

In similar terms he announces, in the preface to the *Philosophy of Money,* the methodological intention to re-examine historical materialism and to find basic societal relationships which make it possible to understand the dynamics of the economic processes in terms of human nature. Simmel states that in the flux of life all social phenomena are a whole and that all aspects of a situation must be taken into consideration. It was the merit of Marx to have pointed out the due place of economic processes among the conditions of civilization. However, economic processes as such can only be understood when the sociologist refers to the psychological and intellectual, moral and spiritual forces that influence the behavior patterns of the economic societies. Simmel has called the consideration of the reciprocity and interdependence of all conditions *the sociological method.* He applied the method in his *Philosophy of Money.* He takes for granted Kapp's theory of money as his economic hypothesis. On this basis, he elaborates most carefully the implications for social conduct which arise in the transition from a natural to a money economy. Simmel analyzes as a sociologist what philosophers have described as a revolutionary change in philosophical conceptions, namely, the elimination of the category of substance in favor of the new scientific thinking in terms of function. In the new credit system the value of money shifts from that of a substance to that of a function. Money becomes a symbol of and an abstraction for values. This new technical device had tremendous repercussions on all ways of life. In a very slow process, this development has promoted the trend toward intellectualism and the spirit of calculation and abstraction as over against the primacy of feelings and of imagination. Simmel analyzes carefully the new attitudes and the new style of life among the ruling classes. Implicitly, he has established the thesis that these new behavior patterns cannot be ascribed to the middle classes in the modern sense. Rather are they the property of the ruling elite in the revolutionary absolute and sovereign state. Simmel rightly characterizes this elite as the first competitive society in which merit and efficiency are higher virtues than birth and fortunes. This, again, is a manifestation of the new pragmatic rationalism and intellectualism. The new economic technique produces positive and negative results. It restricts and levels down original and individual characters. On the other hand, it opens up new avenues to freedom and independence. It emancipates and subjects human beings at the same time. It frees men from the bondage of personal services; it subjects men to the rigidly expanding world of rational and technical institutions.

Unfortunately, the work has never received the recognition which it deserves. It is the sociological pendant to Jacob Burckhardt's *Civilization of the Renaissance in Italy*. It presents under the sociological aspect the problematic character of the modern independence and of the modern individualism after the disintegration of the social system of the feudal societies. Furthermore, Simmel's work remains highly relevant for the critical re-examination of Max Weber's thesis on innerworldly asceticism and on the Puritan spirit. Simmel has made suggestions which point to a quite different solution.

Simmel frequently stated that the sociological method that he applied in this book is universal for all fields in the history of ideas. For the modern man has discovered the impact and pressure of collective institutions on all spheres of human thought and action. He has made this experience a lasting element of his consciousness.[2] . . .

[2] Georg Simmel, *Philosophie des Geldes*, 4th ed. (Leipzig: Duncker und Humblot, 1922).

# SIX

# CULTURE AND LIFE

## RAYMOND ARON

THE ANALYSES contained in *The Philosophy of Money* constitute the transition between the philosophy of sociology and the metaphysics of life. In previous works the two essential themes were those of mass societies and of the function of complex social structures in effecting the liberation of the individual. The liberation of the individual receives further analysis, but in this volume one gets a better idea of the price which it exacts and the situation which it engenders for modern man.

In the past, subjection was more narrow and direct because the individual rendered obedience to other individuals; but today he obeys impersonal and abstract powers.[1] Unlike the serf or gild member of the past, the factory worker of today does not know his master; and the feeling of liberty which he experiences is counterbalanced by the impression of being the slave of things—of enormous and soulless mechanisms.[2] Furthermore, man is increasingly subsumed under function; and orders flow between technician and worker, or between bureaucrat and citizen, rather than between individual and individual.[3]

Moreover, the liberation of the individual can easily degenerate

From "Essai sur la théorie de l'histoire dans l'Allemagne contemporaine," Thèse complementaire pour le doctorat ès lettres, presentée à la Faculté des Lettres de l'Université de Paris par Raymond Aron (Paris: Librairie Philosophique J. Vrin, 1938), Chap. 3, pp. 206-209. Translated by Jon Gower Davies. Reprinted by permission of the publishers.

[1]Georg Simmel, *Philosophie des Geldes* (Leipzig: Duncker und Humblot, 1922), p. 314.

[2] *Ibid.*, pp. 514 ff.

[3] *Ibid.*, pp. 361-65.

into an uprooting.[4] Modern life has the tendency to diminish the individual significance of the beings and objects in the midst of which we live. The circulation of goods, and the possibility of acquiring them all through the use of money, detaches man from all concrete property. The individual has no attachment to the earth, and he is entirely surrounded by an abstract and volatile human world. Consequently he is thrown back onto himself and has to choose between, on the one hand, an unending pursuit of pleasure and, on the other, an effort to grasp that which is of essence in himself.[5]

In his solitude he is crushed by the accomplishments of the collectivity. The accumulated mass of knowledge seems to imply advanced disqualification for the tentative efforts he makes in his attempt to assimilate a portion of that knowledge. His decisions and his acts of will are denied efficacy by the anonymous power of the economy and by the objective laws which regulate the distribution of wealth. Institutions and culture, born of human action, range themselves against their creators.

Simmel returns here[6] to the Marxist theme of the sorcerer's apprentice, with the difference that he talks of *objectification* where Marx more readily talks of *alienation*. Simmel insists on the literal inevitability of the dichotomy established by the process of objectification. Certain extreme situations may permit the individual to lessen the opposition between the objective and the personal culture,[7] but the antinomy is essential and insoluble. To Simmel, Marx's pursuit of the reconstitution of unalienated man would have seemed utopian: and in the attempt by the community to recapture control of the economy, or in the effort to substitute planning and organization for the inevitable operation of the so-called laws of economics, Simmel (if he had considered it to be possible at all) would have seen nothing but another form of tyranny. The individual of today is condemned to be the slave either of things or of the collectivity.

[4] *Ibid.*, pp. 449, 502-503.
[5] *Ibid.*, pp. 532-33.
[6] Georg Simmel, *Der Konflikt der modernen Kultur* (Leipzig: Duncker und Humblot, 1918), p. 4.
[7] Georg Simmel, *Der Krieg und die geistigen Entscheidungen* (Leipzig: Duncker und Humblot, 1917), pp. 58-60.

Why is this conflict insoluble? Why is it tragic? The answer can
be given in a word: because it is at one and the same time metaphysical as well as social. Marx had given a concrete and social
referent to the process by which the spirit expresses and objectifies
itself. Whereas Hegel had already presented the Prussian monarchy
as the event in which the process of objectification was transcended,
Marx reserved [such an event] for postrevolutionary times. Simmel
returns to metaphysics without rediscovering optimism or rationalism, and without exceeding the boundaries of history. The process
of objectification unfolds in the concrete evolution of societies; and
the transcendence of objectification is the destiny of the individual
spirit which pursues integrity by seeking to accomplish its unity in
the face of an inevitable plurality.[8] Metaphysics intervenes only to
delineate the tragedy of the external conflict—i.e., to postulate it
as of the essence of life.

Life is of continuous duration. It is creative spirit; and it is an
effort toward more *of* life and toward more *than* life.[9] It results
in achievements which negate it. Logic, science, law, morality, economics, technology, and so on, are at first but instruments in the
service of life: but these human products tend to free themselves
and to become autonomous; and the logical correspondence of
thought with itself, the truth of knowledge, the legitimacy of acts,
and the expression of good will become ends where once they were
means. Where before one insisted that judgment should be *useful,*
one now insists that it should correspond adequately to the object.
Philosophically, one then goes beyond the psychological interpretation of morality and logic.[10] But with the same step one has introduced into the notion of life the tragedy of duality. In effect, this
universe—once created—obeys its own law, and this law is indifferent to the law of life, even if it does not contradict it. Without pretending to exhaust all the forms of this conflict, let us sketch out
the most important of them.

Human life is individual, and each one of us is first and foremost
a totality. Our qualities, our powers and our riches must necessarily

[8] Georg Simmel, *Philosophische Kultur* (Leipzig: Kröner, 1911), p. 247.
[9] Georg Simmel, *Lebensanchauung* (München and Leipzig: Duncker und
Humblot, 1918), Chap. 1.
[10] *Ibid.,* Chap. 2, particularly pp. 96-98.

be but moments of our being and fragments of our unity. The objectified mind—i.e., the creations accumulated by the species— must be in the service of the objective culture. Furthermore each universe develops according to its own dialectic: the accumulation of discoveries and the progression of knowledge obey an inhuman automatism. As a technician the individual respects nothing but the laws of technology; as a jurist he lives entirely in the world of law; as an artist he knows nothing about anything other than his work, and as a scholar he cares for nothing but the pursuit of truth. In a sense this is one way for man to transcend himself, but at the same time he risks losing himself, for culture should be as unified as the individual, and man realizes himself only in incorporating spiritual objectifications into his life.[11]

The rhythm of objective development and the rhythm of being can never coincide. The objective creations grow without ceasing, while the conditions of existence limit the possibilities of each individual,[12] for although the former (the objective conditions) are offered to all, no one can assimilate them in their entirety. They are rigid; and life is fruitful only when and if it renews itself.

Religious zeal is expressed in dogma, but the dogma will one day cease to express the living faith.[13] The forces of production are arranged in a system which, tomorrow, will prevent the growth of life. In all domains life is condemned to assume forms. Creation implies objectification, and each object is encased in a form. But life must revolt against forms, for forms inhibit the free expansion of life.

[11] Cf. "Der Begriff und die Tragödie der Kultur," in *Philosophische Kultur,* *op. cit.,* pp. 241-77. Also *Lebensanchauung, op. cit.,* pp. 17, 160-61.
[12] *Philosophische Kultur, op. cit.,* pp. 252-53.
[13] *Der Konflikt der modernen Kultur, op. cit.,* pp. 24-25.

# SEVEN

# A CRITIQUE OF SIMMEL'S METHOD

## PITIRIM SOROKIN

. . . Before discussing what is valid in the claims of the formal school, let us indicate at once what is questionable. In the first place, the school's claim that it is a new one is baseless. It is a very old school, perhaps even older than any other school of social science. In the second place, the fundamental discrimination between form and content of social relationship is either fallacious, or represents something on which it is impossible to build sociology as a special science. In the third place, the claim that forms of social relationship are not studied by other than sociological disciplines, is not warranted by the facts. Thus far, Simmel's attempt to build sociology as an autonomous science of the forms of social relationship is not valid. In the fourth place, Simmel and other "formalists" do not keep to their principles, but transgress their own definition, contradict it, and often interpret the same terms in quite different senses. In the fifth place, even if the Simmelian concept of the forms of social relations were true, this would not mean that sociology, as a science of general characteristics of, and the correlation between, social phenomena, could not, or should not, exist. The following considerations will show the validity of these critical propositions.[1]

The claim that the forms of social relationship are not studied by other sciences is not warranted by the facts. It is sufficient to take the science of law in order to see that all Simmel's, or Tönnies', or Vierkandt's, or Richard's, or von Wiese's forms of social relationship

From Pitirim Sorokin, *Contemporary Sociological Theories* (New York: Harper & Row, Publishers, 1928). Copyright 1928 by Harper & Brothers; renewed © 1956 by Pitirim Sorokin. Reprinted by permission of the publishers.

[1] They were formulated already in my *System of Sociology*. See Pitirim Sorokin, *Systema Soziologii* (Petrograd: 1920), Vol. I, pp. 24-35.

have been studied in an excellent and more precise way by the science of law. Is it not evident that such forms as domination and subordination have been always a fundamental object of so-called public, constitutional, or administrative law? The very essence of the phenomena of sovereignty, authority, prestige, power, government, ruling, conflict, domination, subjection, subordination, obedience, together with their forms, origin, and functions have always been one of the fundamental objects of the science of law. And more than that, the science of law, through the Roman jurisconsults, has already given excellent, clear, and brilliant definitions of these phenomena: *Potestas, Majestas, Imperium, Dominus, Princeps, Dignitates, Subjecti,* and so on. Any serious book on constitutional law will show that these forms of social relationship are its principal objects.[2] The same is true of the other forms of formal sociology. If we take international law, we find that such forms of intergroup relationships as contact, isolation, agreement, opposition, conflict, war, and so on, are studied very attentively, and again more clearly, and more formally than is done by the partisans of the formal school. Furthermore, such fundamental forms of social relationship as obligation or duty, dependence, contractual relations, stratification, exploitation, transgression, spoliation, persistence, and continuity, show that all these forms of social relationship have been studied, analyzed, described, classified, and compared by the civil, criminal, processual and other branches of the science of law since immemorial times. All this is so evident that there is no need to insist longer upon it.

What has been said about the science of law may be said of a great many other sciences. They have also studied the forms of social relationship. Take economics. Does it not study division of labor and social differentiation?—cooperation and association?— the forms which Simmel styles *Die Treue* and *Dankbarkeit?*—or that of exploitation and spoliation?—and a great many other forms of

---

[2] See L. Petrajitzky, *Introduction to the Science of Law,* and *Theory of Law and State* (St. Petersburg: 1907, 1909), Vols. I, II; L. Duguit, *Droit constitutionel;* R. Stammler, *Theorie der Rechtswissenschaft* (Halle: 1911); Sohm, *Systematische Rechtswissenschaft* (1906); R. Ihering, *Geist des romischen Rechts,* Vols. I, II, III; T. Mommsen, *Romische Staatsrecht, passim;* H. J. Laski, *Studies in the Problem of Sovereignty* (1917); Pitirim Sorokin, *Theory of Law and State* (1919); B. Kistiakowski, *Social Sciences and Law* (Moscow: 1915); T. Pokrovsky, *Fundamental Problems of Civil Law* (1913).

social relations? ³ Dr. O. Spann is quite right in saying that almost all the laws of economics are quite formal and describe what Simmel styles the forms of relationships.⁴ The same is true in regard to political science, and practically in regard to almost all social sciences. In brief, it is not easy to find a social science which does not study the forms of social relationship in the sense of the formal school, and from a standpoint which is identical with, or similar to, the school's standpoint.

The above means that this claim of the school is not valid. If it is not valid, then the attempt to build sociology on such a claim fails. Since the "forms" are studied by other sciences, there is no room for sociology as a science of the forms of human relationship.

The above explains why, in my opinion, the formal school is very old. Its founders were neither Tönnies nor Simmel, as Dr. Vierkandt claims;⁵ nor Kant, Hegel, Herbart, Ferguson, Fichte, L. von Stein, Gneist, Jellinek, nor Spencer, as G. Richard indicates more rightly.⁶ Its founders were all lawgivers who formulated the first rules of social relations, and especially all jurisconsults and theorizers of law. Beginning at least with Confucius⁷ and the Roman jurisconsults, who so brilliantly formulated the principal forms of social relations, and ending with the theorizers of law, all have been "formal so-

³ To see this it is enough to take any serious course in economics.
⁴ O. Spann rightly indicates that the theory of value describes nothing but a specific form of Simmelian relationship. *"Auch andere national ökonomische Gesetze erweisen sich als rein formale. In Thünens Gesetz der relativen Rationalität der Landbausysteme und ihrer abnehmenden Intensität bei wachsender Entfernung vom Marktorte sind rein 'formale' Beziehungen geschildert. . . . Es muss daher abgelehnt werden, dass die formale Natur des Gegenstandes der von Simmel angestrebten 'Soziologie' alleineigen wäre. Diese fehlt nirgends, und der ganze Gesichtspunkt erweist sich daher als unrichtig."* O. Spann, *Kurzgefasstes System der Gesellschaftslehre* (Leipzig: 1914), pp. 17-19.
⁵ Vierkandt, "Die Überwindung des Positivismus in der deutschen Soziologie der Gegenwart," *Jahrbuch der Soziologie,* B. II., *op. cit.,* p. 1.
⁶ G. Richard, *La Sociologie générale et les lois sociologiques* (Paris, 1912), Chaps. I, IV.
⁷ It is enough to remember Confucius' theory of "the five relationships" and their analysis in the Confucianist teaching to see that a "formal sociology"—and a good one—existed six centuries B.C. See *Li-Kî,* Book I, pp. 62-63; Book VII, p. 3; Book VIII, pp. 1, 15; and *Doctrine of the Mean,* translated in J. Legge's *The Life and Teachings of Confucius* (London: 1895), pp. 313 ff. See also *Policraticus* by John of Salisbury, Books V and VI, where the relationship of domination and subordination is treated in a perfectly formal way.

ciologists." If they are not regarded as the predecessors and the representatives of the formal school, this is probably owing only to the fact that their works have been styled juridical but not sociological. In their character, however, their works, even the very codes of law, beginning with *Corpus Juris Civilis* of Justinian, and ending with new codes of the civil, the constitutional, the criminal, and the processual law (not to mention corresponding theories) are the most brilliant samples of the formal analysis of human relationship or of the forms of social interaction. Their formulas of *Potestas, Imperium, Majestas,* and *Manus* are incomparably better and more formal than the forms of domination in the characteristics of the contemporary formal school. Their formulas of *commercium, consensus, cessio, beneficium,* various *obligationes,* contractual relations, *dominium, proprietas,* and *possessio;* their definitions of the *status libertatis, status civitatis,* and *capitis diminutio;* of marriage, family, consanguinity, inheritance, and so on, represent an "ideal formal sociology" which the formal sociologists may only envy and try to approach as near as possible.

The classification of the social forms of either Tönnies, Simmel, Vierkandt, or von Wiese, is but an incomplete and less formal enumeration of the forms classified, defined, and analyzed in the codes and in the theories of the law. Further, it will be shown that in the classification of the forms of social relations the formal school follows the path trodden by many nonformal sociologists. Hence the conclusions: First, the formal school is a very old one. Second, all great jurisconsults and theorizers of law have been its founders and representatives. Third, the contemporary formal sociologists, contrary to their claim, are less formal in their constructions than the mentioned jurists. Fourth, a further purification of the principles and aspirations of the formal school must lead it to a greater and greater approach to the works of the theorizers of law, and to the codes of law which are nothing but an "ideal formal sociology." If the theories of the present formal school do not coincide completely with the latter, this is owing, as we shall see, to the fact that the formal sociologists are not consistent. They often transgress their own contention of being "formal," and pour into their books a great deal of the "content" of social phenomena.

The above leaves the school in a dilemma: either to be perfect and consistent in its formality, thus becoming nothing but a variety of the theories and codes of law; or to lose its formality and become the kind of "encyclopedic" sociology which is criticized so severely by the formalists. In its present stage, the school represents a mixture of formality and encyclopedism, and, like any imperfect mixture of this kind, it has the shortcomings of both, often without the superiorities of either of these types of sociology.

The school's concepts of form and content are somewhat unsatisfactory also. Since at least the time of Aristotle, philosophical concepts of form and content, or substance, have been very common, and have been given different meanings. Neither Simmel nor his followers, however, have taken care to clarify these somewhat indefinite conceptions. . . . [To] objects which have spatial characteristics these concepts may be applied easily and properly; but how can they be applied to such phenomena as power, authority, domination, subordination, competition, and other forms which do not have geometrically spatial dimensions? Since they have not, it is then clear that to make an analogy between a geometrical form, as a ball, which may be filled by different content, and a social form which may be filled by different content, is rather fallacious. Still more fallacious is it to isolate the social "form" from its content (which in the field of geometrically spatial objects is possible) and then to state that "social forms can remain identical while their members change." [8] We may fill a glass with wine, water, or sugar without changing its form; but I cannot conceive of a social institution whose form would not change when its members, for instance, Americans, were superseded by quite a new and heterogeneous people, e.g., by Chinese or Bushmen. Even if the written constitution of the institution remained untouched on paper, nevertheless its form and organization would change, in direct proportion to how dissimilar the new members were as compared with the previous ones. Quite questionable also is the statement that social form may exist independent of content. Simmel himself has shown that even such a "content-condition" as the number of the members of a

[8] Georg Simmel, "Comment les formes sociales se maintiennent," *L'Année Sociologique,* I. This theory of the persistence of the social group is in its essence nothing but a somewhat shortened and modified theory of the juridical existence of so-called juridical personalities, which was many centuries ago brilliantly elaborated by jurists and lawyers.

group decidedly influences the "form of the group." These examples show how vague are the terminology and analogies of the Simmelian school. In some cases its followers use the concepts of form and content just in this inadmissible "geometrico-spatial" sense. In some other cases, however, they somewhat change their meaning, and use them in the sense of Aristotelian logic, where form designates a broader class of phenomena or concept, while content means a subclass, or a concept which designates this subclass. In this sense the class, and consequently the concept, *human beings,* is a form of the subclasses and corresponding concepts, *man* and *woman,* which may function as content in regard to the human being as a form. The same may be said of an organism, plant, or animal, where *organism* is a form for *plant* and *animal* "content." [9] If such is the logical interrelation of these concepts, then it is clear that they cannot be associated with one another as something logically heterogeneous. With this interpretation, Simmel's claim that sociology studies the forms of social phenomena may mean only that, contrary to other social sciences, sociology studies the most general characteristics of social phenomena which belong to all specific forms of human relationship, while other sciences study these specific characteristics (content). This means that sociology is not a science which studies the specific characteristics of social phenomena, as Simmel claims, but a generalizing science, which Simmel denies. Thus, we come to the conclusion that Simmel's conceptions of form and content are either meaningless and inapplicable to social phenomena; or that they lead to the conception of sociology as a generalizing science, which conception contradicts Simmel's pretensions of building sociology as a specific science.[10]

Furthermore, one who reads attentively the works of Simmel or of the other formalists can easily detect a permanent, sometimes quite a strong alteration, in the meanings which they give to many terms,

[9] Dr. R. Stammler, like Simmel, always uses these terms in his scientific works. On the discrimination of form and content is based his discrimination of law as a form, and economic processes as a content of social life. When, however, Stammler has to define the concepts of form and content, he says that the form means a broader, and the content, a narrower concept for a classification of the same series of phenomena. In other words, form is a *genus;* content is a subclass of the same *genus.* See Stammler, *op. cit.,* pp. 7 ff.; also, *Wirtschaft und Recht, passim.*

[10] Compare Spann, *op. cit.,* pp. 9-19.

and especially to those of form and content. On one page we are told that the object matter of sociology is the forms of human relationship; a few lines or pages further on, we are suddenly told that this object is the forms of socialization! [11] Nevertheless, these two concepts of the forms of human relations, and the forms of socialization mean something quite different. The forms of human relationship may mean not only the forms of socialization, but those of desocialization also; not only association, but dissociation; not only cooperation, but warfare, also.[12] If we define sociology as the science of the forms of human relationship, then the processes of dissociation, opposition, conflict, and warfare must be included in the field of its study. If we define it as a science of the forms of socialization, then these processes, as opposed to those of socialization, must be excluded from the field of sociology. For Simmel and some of the Simmelists, this heterogeneity of the two definitions does not exist. They use them interchangeably, and without any attempt to reconcile them. This naturally results in a series of logical inconsistencies, and in a vagueness of theoretical constructions.

What has been said of the fundamental conceptions of Simmelian sociology may be said of its many other propositions. Although valuable in some respects, they are stamped by the same vagueness, indefiniteness, changeable meanings, and often by a purely specu-

---

[11] See Georg Simmel, *Soziologie*, pp. 4 ff.; *Grundfragen der Soziologie*, pp. 22 ff. It is curious to note that one of the recent propagandists of Simmelianism in this country, being quite accurate in his characterization of Simmel's theory, makes such a shifting of meaning in the following way: "This concept of society as form, or rather of the form of the socialization," and so on. Nicholas J. Trykman, *The Social Theory of Georg Simmel* (Chicago: University of Chicago Press, 1925). The author, like Simmel, seems not to see that "forms of human relationship" and the "forms of socialization" mean something quite different and by "simple" or "rather" it is impossible to jump from one to another and identify their meaning. See the whole of Book I, in Spykman's quoted work where he, like Simmel, uses interchangeably these two definitions.

[12] E. A. Ross and E. Dupréel, who, independent of Simmel, have very ably tried to outline the concept of sociology as a science of human relations, and who give one of the best analyses of human relations, are free from this *quaternio terminorum* of Simmel and the Simmelian school. See E. A. Ross, *Principles of Sociology*, Part III; E. Dupréel, *Le rapport social, Essai sur l'objet et la méthode de la sociologie* (Paris: 1912), Chap. 4 and *passim*. See also his "Sociologie et psychologie," *Institut Solvay, Bullétin mensuel* (January 1911), 180-86. Ross and Dupréel, being relationists in sociology, do not belong to the formal school.

lative character. In this respect they are still in the stage of a purely philosophical or speculative sociology.[13]

Finally, the insufficiency of formal sociology is shown also by the transgression of its principles by the formalists themselves. In spite of their severe criticism of the "encyclopedic" sociology, their own works have the same "encyclopedic character." They are "contaminated" by a great deal of the "social content" poured into their "forms." Dr. Vierkandt's book may serve as an example. In spite of Vierkandt's declaration that he is going to deal only with the forms of social phenomena, he fails to carry on his program. Beginning with the second chapter, the book (pp. 58-179) is filled with the "content"; with a long discussion of human instincts (of self-feeling, subordination, of mutual help, pugnacity, sympathy, and so on), together with their modification in the process of interaction; with sketches of the history of family, professional groups, classes, orders, nations, and states; with a philosophy of social unity and reality; and with imitation, suggestion, mob-mind, and so on—in brief, with the usual "stuff" found in all nonformal sociological books. With

[13] From a purely methodological standpoint, Simmel's sociological method lacks scientific method. I must express my complete disagreement with Dr. R. Park's or Dr. Spykman's high estimation of the sociological method of Simmel. Besides the above logical deficiency, Simmel's method entirely lacks either experimental approach, quantitative investigation, or any systematic factual study of the discussed phenomena. In vain one would look in his work for a systematic method like that of the Le Play school, or of the methodological principles of social sciences developed by A. Cournot in his *Considérations sur la marche des idées,* and so on; *Essai sur le fondements de nos connaissances; Traité de l'enchainement des idées fondamentales dans les sciences et dans l'histoire;* or some principles like those of H. Rickert and W. Windelband concerning the classification of sciences and of their methods of generalizing (nomographic or nomothetic) and individualizing (ideographic) sciences; or something like Max Weber's method of the "ideal typology"; or Galton's, Pearson's, and A. Tchuproff's quantitative methods of investigation; or even a simple, careful, and attentive study of the facts he is talking about. All this is lacking. What there is represents only the speculative generalization of a talented man, backed by the "method of illustration" in the form of two or three facts incidentally taken and often one-sidedly interpreted. Without Simmel's talent the same stuff would appear poor. Simmel's talent saves the situation, but only as far as talent compensates for lack of scientific methodology. Under such conditions, to call the sociologists "back to Simmel," as Drs. Park and Spykman do, means to call them back to a pure speculation, metaphysics, and a lack of scientific method. Speculation and metaphysics are excellent things in their proper places, but to mix these with the science of sociology means to spoil each of those sciences.

a modification, the same may be said of all the works of the formal
school. I do not know any one which would not have an "encyclopedic character," and in which the data of biology, ethnology,
anthropology, history, psychology, political science, economics, and
literature, are not mixed and used. In brief, "the sin of encyclopedism" is as common within the formal sociology as within the
nonformal sociology it criticizes.[14]

The above should be sufficient to show that the formal school has
failed to build sociology as an "autonomous and independent
science" on the discrimination of the categories of form and content. To this it is possible to add that even the attempt itself to build
such an independent science of sociology or of any other science, as
far as it pretends to be something more than a mere conditional and
approximate limitation of its field for the sake of a mere practical
conveniency, is rather fallacious. Many sociologists[15] seem to be very
anxious to construct such "an independent sociology." For this purpose they are ready to prohibit all sociologists from using the data
and the materials used by other sciences. They dream of a "pure"
sociology, absolutely independent from, and not contaminated with,
the data of other sciences. To achieve this fantastic goal they write
and publish hundreds of volumes filled with a discussion of what
sociology, as an independent science, ought to be, how it ought to be
built, and how it ought to be separated from all other sciences. I
confess that I find almost all such reasoning fruitless. If an author
knows a wonderful secret about building such a sociology, let him
show the validity of his secret by its factual building, but not by a
mere reasoning of "how scientific sociology ought to be built." The
success of his factual building is a much more convincing argument
in favor of his secret than mere reasoning.[16] As a matter of fact, these

[14] This makes baseless the pretension of formal sociology to play the same role
for other social sciences which is played by mathematics or physical mechanics
in regard to other physical and technical sciences. Neither the pretension nor
the analogy are justified in any way.

[15] See for instance F. Znaniecki, "The Object Matter of Sociology," *American
Journal of Sociology* (January 1927). See also Spann, *op. cit.*, pp. iv, vii, Chap. 1
and *passim*.

[16] Pareto, who devotes only five lines to his definition of sociology in his fifteen-
hundred page treatise on the subject, and Ross, who in his *Principles of Sociology* does not give any definition of sociology, but starts at once to build it,
proceed much better than all those who extensively discuss what sociology is,
and by this discussion complete their "books."

reasonings are only a proof of the helplessness of such an author. Likewise, the attempt itself to build "an independent sociology" is rather fallacious. There is practically no science (except perhaps mathematics and formal logic) which is independent and "uncontaminated" by data taken from other sciences. I do not know any chemistry which would not use the data of physics, or even of biology. I do not know any biology which would not use the data of chemistry, physics, or some other sciences. There is no anatomy which does not contain the data of physiology, ecology, systematics, histology, or whatever. Various branches of physical, chemical, and biological sciences are so closely interwoven and mixed and some of them, like organic or colloidal chemistry, are such a *mixtum compositum* of different sciences that only by completely ignoring their real character is it possible to dream of "an absolutely independent science." The same mixture of data and premises is still more conspicuous in the field of social sciences, or those which deal with human beings. I cannot imagine psychology without the data of biology, anatomy, and physiology. I have not seen any important treatise in economic or political sciences which did not use the data of psychology, biology, history, demography, ethics, or even philosophy.[17] More than that, practically all the most important books in

[17] A sociologist cannot be troubled much by the divergency of the existing definitions of sociology. This situation is not worse than that of the economists, historians, theorizers of law, and psychologists, or the students of any other of the cultural sciences. All these sciences still wait for their definition, and are understood in very different ways. An illustration of this is given by the papers of the most prominent economists, published in *The Trend of Economics* (New York: 1924). The volume conspicuously shows that there are as many different definitions of economics as there are economists. The most modern definition of it is that "economics is a science of behavior." (Wesley C. Mitchell, *ibid.*, pp. 22 ff.) Psychology is defined now also as a science of human behavior, as is sociology. Thus, if we must be guided by definitions of "pure" sciences, psychology, economics and sociology cannot exist, because they are all "sciences of behavior." Is it necessary to add that such independent sciences do not exist indeed; but, on the other hand, the identity of the definitions does not hinder the study of the phenomena of human behavior from somewhat various standpoints; and in somewhat different combinations, which give a basis for a relative and conditional separation of these disciplines. In all these respects, the situation of sociology is not worse than that of these cultural sciences. It is worse only in the sense that while economics and psychology have been busy with the study of facts, sociologists have greatly wasted their time in a discussion of the "object matter of pure sociology." But, luckily for us, now they also are dropping this fruitless business, and are getting busy with factual study.

cultural, psychological, and social sciences, even in biology, have been those which have been rich in such a mixture of the data of various sciences. Whether I take *Philosophy of Zoology,* by Lamarck, or *The Origin of Species,* by Darwin, I find it difficult to decide exactly to what branch of science these works belong. The data of various, even of social sciences, are so mixed in such works that it is not easy to decide the question. At any rate they do not belong to the kind of "formal and independent works" of which "sociological autonomists" dream. The same is still more true in regard to the epoch-making works in the field of cultural and social sciences. Whether we take *The Republic* of Plato, or *The Politics* of Aristotle, *La Scienza Nuova* by Vico, *Discourse on Livy* by Machiavelli, Montesquieu's *The Spirit of Law,* Malthus' *Essay on Population,* or the works of Adam Smith, Saint-Simon, I. Kant, Auguste Comte, H. Spencer, and so on—all these great works are composed from, and on the basis of, the data of various sciences, to such an extent that we cannot say exactly to what "department" of science—economics, or sociology, or philosophy, or psychology, or political science—they really belong. On the other hand, I do not know any formal work which has produced anything above an average scholastic value. For these reasons I do not see why sociologists need to have "an absolutely independent sociology" not contaminated by the data of other sciences, and not overlapping their fields. Neither do I see how such a fantastic goal could be achieved, whether in the field of sociology or of any other science. I do not believe that such a formalism can produce anything valuable. The attempt sacrifices the real unity of human knowledge to purely accidental and practical subdivisions required by "departmental subdivisions," and by other similar needs external to science itself. This means that the very attempt of formal sociology to build "an independent sociology" is rather fallacious.[18]

[18] The same is true of the recent attempt of Professor F. Znaniecki to define the "object matter of sociology." After his severe criticism of all "hodgepodge" sociologies instead of a "pure" sociology he gave an additional "hodgepodge" conception of sociology as a science of human interinfluence and relationship, which embraces criminology, ethics, educational theory, political science, and so on. It is evident that the conception has all the sins of other "hodgepodge" definitions so severely criticized by the author. Nevertheless, such a sin is better than the "purity" of the "pure" sociologists, which has never been attained by anybody. For my part, as far as some guiding and approximate definition of sociology is necessary, I find the most suitable definition of it as a science of the

The above, however, does not mean that the formal school has been quite fruitless in sociology. Through its analysis of human relations and their types it has contributed something valuable to a definite part of sociology in *systematizing human relations and social processes*. The multitude of concrete human relationships and the complexity of social processes make it necessary to classify them into a few large classes, with further subdivisions, in this way preventing us from becoming lost in a wild forest of interrelations. Like zoological or botanical systematics, sociology must have, among its parts, at least an approximate classification of social relationships in order to make orientation possible in the vast field of social phenomena. For this part of sociology, the formal school, with its consideration of "the forms of human relations" and with its efforts to classify them, has contributed something valuable. However, in this respect also, the school must share its contributions with other sociological schools which have contributed to this field, at any rate no less than the formal school. It is enough to remember H. Spencer's discrimination of the processes of social growth, differentiation and integration, and dissolution and disintegration; or G. Tarde's fundamental classification of social processes into three groups: *repetition, opposition,* and *adaptation* or *invention;* in order to see that neither Tönnies, Simmel, nor any other partisans of the formal school could be regarded as the initiator in the classification of social relations and processes. Even the detailed table of Dr. von Wiese, in its three principal divisions of human relations—*toward* each other, *away* from each other, and *mixed*—follows pretty closely Tarde's classification, but not that of Simmel. Similarly, von Wiese's classification of social processes: *differentiation, integration,* and *destruction,* is but a slightly changed classification of H. Spencer. These indications are enough to show that even in this field the contribution of the formal school does not represent a monopoly. . . .

---

most general characteristics common to all classes of social phenomena and the correlations which exist between these classes. However, several other definitions are as good as this, and I do not think it is necessary to argue much about them. It is much better to "build" than to argue about "how to build." See Znaniecki, *op. cit.,* pp. 558-84.

# PART FOUR

# SIMMEL'S CURRENT INFLUENCE
# ON AMERICAN SOCIOLOGY

SIMMEL'S INFLUENCE in American sociology is at present perhaps most pronounced in the fields of small-group research and in social conflict theory. This is why examples from these two areas were chosen for this section—even though Simmel's heritage could be shown to have been fruitful in other areas as well.

Theodore M. Mills, of Yale University, has self-consciously utilized a number of Simmel's original leads in his work. His paper reprinted here is only one of several in which he makes systematic use of Simmel's brilliant and unsystematic ideas.

The second paper, by the editor, is part of his *The Functions of Social Conflict*, a book in which Simmel's notions on social conflict are examined, extended, and confronted with theoretical and empirical findings which have become available since his days.

# ONE

# SOME HYPOTHESES ON
# SMALL GROUPS FROM SIMMEL

## THEODORE M. MILLS

PARTLY FROM A growing impression that Simmel's conceptions of group process have yet to be incorporated into our more general sociological theories and partly out of curiosity, I select . . . several notions representing his theoretical interests, reformulate them as hypotheses, attempt to specify the appropriate variables, and suggest briefly how they may be tested experimentally. That Simmel did not test his propositions by a similar procedure does not mean that it is foreign to his purposes; by one incisive example after the other and by continual return to, and revision of, a theme, he worked carefully toward closer approximations of what he considered universal properties of social processes. The techniques of experimentation are different, but its aim need not be. With imaginative experiments there is the possibility of attaching to a proposition an estimate of the probability that it is true. I have chosen a few of Simmel's statements for detailed consideration rather than present the fuller array that might reflect more accurately the variety of his interests.

### PLAY-FORM AND GROUP PROCESS

"The more profound, double sense of 'social game' is that not only [is] the game . . . played in society . . . but that, with its help, people actually 'play society.' " [1]

From *The American Journal of Sociology*, LXIII, No. 6 (May 1958), 642-50, Reprinted by permission of the author and the publishers, The University of Chicago Press.

[1] Kurt H. Wolff (ed.), *The Sociology of Georg Simmel* (New York: The Free Press of Glencoe, Inc., 1950).

From this notion of Simmel's and from the subsequent one—that we may understand more fully societal forces at work by analyzing the sociological form of its play—I would like to develop in this first section two hypotheses for possible test in the small-group laboratory. One hypothesis deals with the ability to play in any form (some groups can only play; some work while at play); the other involves four mechanisms used by groups to translate their group life into play-form.

There is, according to Simmel, a two-way relationship between the processes of the day-to-day group and the game, the party, social play, and other instances of "sociability." The first is that play-form is clearly and emphatically dissociated and autonomous from other affairs of the group; the second, that basic issues in the life of the group are represented in its form of play, either directly, or inversely, by their negation or some other mechanism. In respect to the first, Simmel writes:

> Actual forces, needs, impulses of life produce the forms of our behavior that are suitable for play. These forms, however, become independent contents and stimuli within play *itself or, rather, as* play. . . . All these forms are lifted out of the flux of life and freed of their material with its inherent gravity. On their own decision, they choose or create the objects in which they prove or embody themselves in their purity. This is what gives play both its gaeity and the symbolic significance by which it is distinguished from mere joke. . . . It is from their [art and play] origin, which keeps them permeated with life, that they draw their depth and strength. . . . Yet their significance and their very nature derive from that fundamental change through the forms engendered by the purposes and materials of life, are separated from them, and themselves become the purpose and the material for their own existence. From the realities of life they take only what they . . . can absorb in their autonomous existence.[2]

And further:

> All the forms of interaction or sociation among men—the wish to outdo, exchange, the formation of parties, the desire to wrest something from the other, the hazards of accidental meetings and separations, the change between enmity and cooperation, the overpowering by ruse and revenge—in the seriousness of reality, all of these are imbued with

[2] *Ibid.,* p. 42.

purposive contents. In the game they lead their own lives; they are propelled exclusively by their own attraction.[3]

This tacit understanding that play is not work, fantasy, not fact, and make-believe, not reality, gives these forms enough freedom so that they can reflect reality, fact, and the issues at work in the group. In designating "sociability," or the social game, as the play-form of social interaction, Simmel suggests that its connection to these interactions is similar to the relationship of art to reality and that its task is "to make the joining and breaking up of sociated individuals the exact reflection of the relations among these individuals." [4] It "transfers the serious, often tragic character of these problems into symbolic play of its shadowy realm which knows no frictions, since shadows, being what they are, cannot collide." [5] It "is spared the frictions with reality by its merely formal relationship to it. Yet, because of this, it derives from reality, even to the mind of the more sensitive person, a significance and a symbolic, playful richness of life that are the greater, the more perfect [the play-form] is." [6]

Everett C. Hughes calls Simmel "the Freud of the study of society." [7] One can agree with him if Simmel's initial insight that certain group processes are most clearly reflected in symbolic forms of play proves as useful as Freud's conviction that unconscious motives of the individual are revealed in dreams and fantasies. Yet in one respect Simmel leaves off where Freud went to work. Aside from a few additional hints and several strikingly clear illustrations, he developed the matter no further. The necessary tools are lacking —a schema for analyzing the form of group process, a similar one for the sociological study of forms of play, and a set of guides for translating from one to the other. Nonetheless, from the few hints, I shall try to extend his exploration by setting up several guiding hypotheses I think can be investigated empirically.

*The capacity to create, or to participate in, forms of play.* Simmel conceived of "thresholds" for play. If these are too low, and if they

[3] *Ibid.,* p. 49.
[4] *Ibid.,* p. 54.
[5] *Ibid.*
[6] *Ibid.,* p. 44.
[7] Georg Simmel, *Conflict: The Web of Group Affiliations,* translated by Kurt Wolff and Reinhard Bendix (New York: The Free Press of Glencoe, Inc., 1955), Foreword by Hughes.

are crossed, the distinction between reality and play is dissolved; the dissociation which gives play its symbolic character breaks down. In effect, the audience shoots the villain; or, in Simmel's illustration, the reaction to coquetry destroys its artfulness:

> As long as [the man] rejects [coquetry's] attractions or . . . is its mere victim [who] without any will of his own is dragged along by its vascillations between a half "yes" and a half "no," coquetry has not yet assumed for him a form that is commensurate with sociability. . . . It does not attain [this] until he asks for no more than this freely suspended play which only dimly reflects the erotically definitive as a remote symbol; [not] until he is no longer attracted by the lust for the erotic element or by fear of it.[8]

Presumably, the threshold is crossed when unresolved issues, associated with other contexts and aroused by symbols in play, control the person. Pressing needs obliterate the boundary between work and play, making the latter an occasion for acting on these needs.

> Sociability [or play] also shies away from the entirely subjective and purely inwardly spheres of [one's] personality. Discretion which is the first condition of sociability in regard to one's behavior toward others is equally . . . required in regard to one's dealing with oneself: in both cases, its violation causes the sociological art form of sociability to degenerate into a sociological naturalism. . . . These thresholds are passed both when individuals interact from motives of objective content and purpose and when their entirely personal and subjective aspects make themselves felt.[9]

Groups, as well as individuals, have play thresholds. The first hypothesis is that the level of the threshold is a function of the group's capability for meeting external and internal demands satisfactorily (as defined by the standards of the group). As external demands and internal strains increase for a group, we can predict lower thresholds; eventually the unresolved issues will spill over, transforming play into problem-solving. And, as we move from one type of group to another—from the effective, versatile, well-organized group possessing a common basis for resolving new problems and meeting new demands to groups that are unsuccessful, rigid, emotionally distressing, and lacking the capacity for new solutions

---

[8] Wolff, *op. cit.*, p. 51.
[9] *Ibid.*, p. 47.

to problems as well as a means of working through differences—as we move along this continuum, we expect increasing difficulty both in dissociating work from play and in creating sociologically and psychologically significant forms of play. Just as an estimate of a person's sexual and social maturity is his artfulness at the game of coquetry, so an estimate of a group's resources is its ability to "leave" itself and play itself.

*Symbolic mechanisms.* Another estimate of a group's resources may prove to be the kind of mechanism it employs in playing itself. By taking certain liberties in interpreting Simmel, I present four symbolic mechanisms which may explain connections between the ordinary processes of the group and its play-form. By taking still greater liberties, I arrange them in order—from those likely to be employed by effective and integrated groups to those likely to be used by groups in a state of disintegration. Simmel's suggestion that these connections are similar to the relation of art to reality is instructive here. On the one hand, it encourages specification of the mechanisms, but, on the other, it warns against assuming that only a few exist. As a beginning, I offer the following four.

1. In its play-form the group recreates characteristics of group processes which have been, and are, its principal sources of effectiveness, of gratification, and of pride. For example, in playing "house," children recreate family roles and relationships, boys' clubs establish an authority structure and give themselves surnames, and therapy groups in their "coffee hours" elect from their ranks a substitute leader as a source of security and of pride. Repeated in the game of charades is the sense of accomplishment in having overcome communication blocks, and repeated in the dance is the joint kinesthetic pleasure of man and woman moving together. By its mode of abstraction, this mechanism enables members to relive and enjoy the essentials of certain group processes and in this way elaborate their sources of enjoyment. Moreover, since the play-form itself is a new and separate part of group culture, reflecting certain essentials of the group, the mechanism provides a new cultural object of group identification. New pride can be taken in the play-form.

2. The group in its play-form recreates characteristics of group process which have been and are the principal sources of strain. Competition and its associated "wish to outdo . . . desire to wrest

something from the other [and] . . . overpowering by ruse and revenge" [10] are duplicated in warlike games in which power is represented by numbers, aristocratic rank, and combinations of these. Room is left for skill, ruse, and deceit, but aptitude in these respects does not alone determine gain or loss. Restrictions on self-revelation and limits to frankness are duplicated in play-forms which place high value upon being able to assess what the other has in his "hand." Moreover, deviant members of the group are invited as playmates. Though this mechanism still maintains the boundary between group process and the play-form, it presents in disguised form the problematic issues of group life and presents them, in a sense, "out there," where they may be observed and possibly comprehended. In another sense, it presents them "here" to be participated in, experimented with, played with. One's role in respect to these processes may be rehearsed, revised, and reintegrated with his other functions in the group. It is analogous to the more self-conscious process of psychodrama,[11] and perhaps also to interaction in individual and group psychotherapy (though the issues in the three cases may be entirely different).

3. The group in its play-form adopts features which stand in contrast to its regular features. Ambiguity of norms is replaced by rigidly circumscribed patterns of play; there is a rule for every conceivable contingency. In other instances, reticence is replaced by obligations to be open and friendly. Prohibited exchanges of information become appropriate, and suppressed feelings may be expressed. As Simmel suggests, "A characteristically sociable . . . trait is the courtesy with which the strong and extraordinary individual not only makes himself equal to the weaker, but even acts as if the weaker were the more valuable and superior." [12] Though here again play-form is determined largely by sources of group strain, two important (and unique) functions are performed by the contrasting features: (1) tension may be expressed and reduced through acting upon the principles and patterns which represent the antithesis of the sources of high tension; but (2), perhaps even more important,

[10] *Ibid.*, p. 49.

[11] J. L. Moreno, *Who Shall Survive?* rev. ed. (Beacon, N.Y.: Beacon House, Inc., Publishers, 1953).

[12] Wolff, *op. cit.*, p. 49.

in creating and incorporating this inverse picture of itself, the group extends its culture to encompass not only what the group *is* but precisely that which it is *not*. Instead of observing, rehearsing, or experimenting with problematical issues, the group creates a fantasy. Yet, once created, acted on, and solidified into the play-form of the group, the fantasy becomes a part of group culture and, therefore, a component of the object of group identification. Compared to those above, this mechanism indicates that a group has more serious unresolved issues and a lower threshold for play, in Simmel's sense.

4. The group in its play-form negates the problematic processes of group life. Status tension is denied and replaced by the principle of equality—designated by number or other universalistic signs—and assured by systematic rotation, the game being incomplete until all players assume all possible positions. The deviant member is less likely to be invited to the party. In other instances, games of chance negate the part played by individual skill, technical accomplishment, and special abilities in determining outcomes in the regular group. In substituting logical, mathematical, or other related principles for social ones, this mechanism protects members from associating in any way elements of work with elements of play. At the same time it probably detracts from enjoyment by eliminating the reverberations of regular group process. Group issues are kept at great distance, just as distant as the erotic element in the Platonic relationship. The function of the mechanism is to defend a diminishing threshold.

The second hypothesis is that, as groups become less able to cope with their external and internal demands and as the threshold for dissociating group life from play becomes lower, there is a tendency for groups to shift from the first through to the fourth mechanism. Correspondingly, as demands are increased in proportion to the capacity of a given group, a similar shift occurs.

*Empirical tests.* A group's capability for meeting internal and external demands is the independent variable in the two hypotheses. It may be varied systematically by screening, matching, and differentially classifying groups according to their demonstrated performance in response to tasks. Demands may be increased within a given set of groups by presenting them with tasks and situations, graduated in their difficulty and in their emotional involvement. Moreover, demands may be concentrated in specific areas of group process.

Ease and difficulty in communication, for example, can most easily be varied by using the Bavelas baffle board employed by Leavitt;[13] success and failure in response to external demands may be varied by reports from the experimenter;[14] problems regarding authority relations and intermember relations may be induced by trained, role-playing leaders and members;[15] finally, by selection according to basic interpersonal reflexes, values, personality needs, or libidinal ties, other demands may be induced and varied systematically. These are but a few available techniques for establishing degrees of strain in specified areas of group process.

The dependent variables in the hypotheses are the play threshold and the mechanisms. A variety of play situations may aid in developing adequate measures of these variables: groups may be asked (*a*) to create a game which they then play; (*b*) to select a game to play; (*c*) to re-enact a drama in which the issues either correspond to, negate, or represent a reversal of issues in their working group; (*d*) to exchange roles in re-enacting their own process; or, finally, (*e*) to create group fantasies.[16] Estimates of resistance to play are needed, and further progress is required in our analysis of the organizing principles of games,[17] of expressive behavior in role-play, and, in the last case, of the sociological facets of fantasy material.[18]

Strategically, following up these notions of Simmel's promises at least two contributions. First, play-form reflects not only the existence of certain issues but, as a product of the whole group—a

[13] H. J. Leavitt, "Some Effects of Certain Communication Patterns on Group Performance," *Journal of Abnormal and Social Psychology*, XLVI (1951), 38-50.

[14] J. W. Thibaut, "An Experimental Study of the Cohesiveness of Underprivileged Groups," *Human Relations*, III (1950), 251-78.

[15] Kurt Lewin and Ronald Lippitt, "An Experimental Approach to the Study of Autocracy and Democracy," in A. Paul Hare, Edgar F. Borgatta, and Robert F. Bales (eds.), *Small Groups* (New York: Alfred A. Knopf, Inc., 1955), pp. 516-23.

[16] W. E. Henry and H. Guetzkow, "Group Projection Sketches for the Study of Small Groups," *Journal of Social Psychology*, XXXIII (1951), 77-102.

[17] See Ethel M. Riddle, "Aggressive Behavior in a Small Social Group," in Hare, Borgatta, and Bales (eds.), *op. cit.*, pp. 35-37, for a résumé of an analysis of poker play.

[18] T. M. Mills, "Sign Process Analysis." Unpublished Ph.D. thesis presented at Harvard University, 1952.

product that has been created or accepted through a process of give and take, rejection, selection, and amalgamation—it reflects the relative importance of issues. As a group product, it represents a balance of group forces—a kind of balance that is difficult to deduce from answers to an array of discrete questions. According to Simmel, it "may more completely, constantly, and realistically reveal the deepest nature of [group] reality than could any attempt at grasping it more directly." [19] Second, a fuller understanding of the symbolic connections among play-form, fantasy, and so on, and group process may strengthen the role of leaders of therapy, training, and discussion groups in assessing, not personal motivation, but the salience of issues confronting the group as a whole.

## COMPARATIVE DYNAMICS OF DYADS AND TRIADS

In the translated works of Simmel there are over sixteen propositions contrasting the dynamics of small, undifferentiated systems with larger, differentiated ones. Though he fails, often, to specify the boundaries between the two types, he employs throughout his discussion the abstract models of the two-element and three-element systems. For the purpose of this section I apply his propositions solely to the two- and three-person groups and present several hypotheses which, in my interpretation, summarize the chief line of his argument.[20]

Concerning dyads and triads, he suggests: (1) that, while an impending sense of death of the relationship permeates the two-person group, a sense of permanency exists in the triad;[21] (2) that dyads lack but triads possess an object which represents to its mem-

[19] Wolff, *op. cit.*, p. 56.

[20] For studies on the effect of group size see Hare, Borgatta, and Bales (eds.), *op. cit.*, pp. 665-66, for a list of references; also Robert F. Bales, A. Paul Hare, and Edgar Borgatta in Joseph Gittler (ed.), *Review of Sociology* (New York: John Wiley & Sons, 1957), chap. xii; and Philip E. Slater, "Contrasting Correlates of Group Size," to be published in *Sociometry*. For studies of three-person groups see Theodore M. Mills, "Power Relations in Three-Person Groups," in Dorwin Cartwright and Alvin Zander (eds.), *Group Dynamics* (Evanston, Ill.: Row-Peterson, 1953), pp. 428-42; and other references listed by W. E. Vinacke and A. Arkoff, "An Experimental Study of Coalitions in the Triad," *American Sociological Review*, XXII (1957), 406-14.

[21] Wolff, *op. cit.*, p. 124.

bers the relationship as a whole or the collectivity;[22] (3) that in the dyad affection may culminate in intimacy but that in the three-person group it tends to be either checked or restricted to a sub-part;[23] (4) that delegation of functions on universalistic criteria cannot be easily accomplished in the two-part group, as it can in the triad;[24] (5) that scapegoating disintegrates the dyad, while it may serve temporarily as a rebuilding expedient in the triad;[25] and (6) that the assumption on the part of one member of a supraindividual role, representing the relationship itself, expells a single partner, but it need not in the case of two partners.[26]

Concerning small and large systems, Simmel suggests: (1) that small systems tend "to burn up all their energy," while larger ones maintain residual strength;[27] (2) that, while decisive stands must be taken in smaller systems, in larger ones the group as a whole may suspend many;[28] (3) that norms cover a wider range of behavior in small than in large systems but incorporate a broader range of tolerance; (4) that small, undifferentiated groups contain no subpart which mediates between the individual and the collectivity;[29] (5) that stress in the small system results either in solidification or in collapse, while it tends to reduce the larger system into two-part systems;[30] (6) that small groups possess means for handling complex conflicts between persons, while larger ones, lacking this faculty, are more capable of controlling conflicts between organized subunits;[31] (7) that in small systems reintegrating mechanisms are limited chiefly either to keeping faith until positive forces reappear or to altering the norms, as illustrated by the comment, "We no longer talk about that," whereas larger systems can reorganize so as to minimize conflict and maintain a constant boundary in respect to its external situation;[32] (8) that, on the reciprocity assumption, one party's

[22] *Ibid.*, p. 123.
[23] *Ibid.*, p. 126.
[24] *Ibid.*, p. 134.
[25] *Ibid.*, p. 152.
[26] *Ibid.*, p. 36.
[27] *Ibid.*, p. 92.
[28] *Ibid.*
[29] *Ibid.*, p. 97.
[30] *Conflict* . . . , *op. cit.*, p. 65.
[31] *Ibid.*, p. 67.
[32] *Ibid.*, p. 67.

cathexis (and related affective attributes such as reticence or self-revelation, faithful or unfaithfulness, gratitude or ingratitude, frankness or deceit) largely determines the nature of the undifferentiated system, whereas in differentiated ones, contrary affective relationships may not only exist side by side but also share in a common conception of the collectivity;[33] and, finally, to interpolate from Simmel, (9) that, since it is easier to elicit certain behavior from one party to oneself than to induce certain behavior between other parties, group process is less determined by a single party's needs in the larger system than in the smaller, undifferentiated one.

Let me not only subsume all these propositions under models of the dyad and the triad but also extract, with no intention of exhausting Simmel's argument, a major theme to serve as a guide in our comparative study. The hypothesis is that over a wide array of tasks and situations, and with increasing pressure from external demands, the two-person group tends to readjust at a lower level of integration than the three-person group.

Initial qualifications are necessary. If we take as a working hypothesis Bales's proposition that an inverse relationship exists between (1) the expenditure of resources upon adaptive and goal attainment problems and (2) internally disorganizing tendencies,[34] we should expect both two- and three-person groups to exhibit negatively sloped curves, where degree of external pressure is represented along the $x$ axis and level of group integration along the $y$ axis. The first qualification is that the negative slope of the curve for two-person groups is greater than the negative slope of the three-person groups, and, second, at some undetermined point they intersect.

The dyad, lacking the variety of reintegrating mechanisms, tends to decompose more readily in response to increasing demands than the triad; yet, as external demands diminish, the dyad, with its capacity for intimacy, and so on, is capable of attaining a higher level of integration than the three-person group. . . .

In spite of the limitations of our measures of group integration, the careful modern experimenter might test the hypothesis, particu-

[33] *Ibid.*, p. 67.
[34] Robert F. Bales, *Interaction Process Analysis* (Cambridge, Mass.: Addison-Wesley Press, 1950).

larly if he induces emphatically different degrees of external pressure.

*Changes in membership.* Simmel, with characteristic perspicacity, warns against the simple conclusion that all pairs or all threesomes function in the same way. Under some conditions the addition of a new member solidifies the dyad (as a child often unites parents), while in other circumstances it separates them (as illustrated in the warning, "If you want to lose your friend, introduce him to your sister"). Still, under other conditions, as observed by Spiegel, the newcomer may be used, in his relations to the others, to absorb the unresolved issues of the original pair.[35] Simmel illustrates these processes but fails to specify the conditions under which we might expect one pattern or another. Let me suggest two experimental procedures which may contribute to a more useful formulation of the dynamics of pairs and threesomes.

Properties of the dyad may be assessed by comparing the way it absorbs a newcomer with assimilation processes in groups of three or more.[36] Moreover, newcomers may be introduced into a series of differentially composed pairs (selection being on the basis of faithfulness, gratitude, conflict, reticence, or deceit, as Simmel might propose, or on the basis of sex, status, complementarity of needs, values, or interpersonal anxieties and defenses). How do attributes of pairs affect the dynamics of taking in a new member? What sorts of pairs tend to unite, tend to separate, tend to transfer conflict into relations with the newcomer? Do affective, behavioral, and cognitive aspects of the original dyad change together, or do they change differentially? Moreover, in respect to the hypothesis above, is there the expected increase in variety and effectiveness of integrative mechanisms? How does integrative capacity compare between variously composed original pairs? Finally, under increasing external pressure, how do the curves for these groups compare with the curve for three-person groups mentioned above?

Though not so fully discussed by Simmel, the expedient of taking

[35] John Spiegel, "The Resolution of Role-Conflict in the Family," *Psychiatry*, XX (1957), 1-16.
[36] See Theodore M. Mills *et al.*, *Group Structure and the Newcomer* (Oslo: Oslo University Press, 1957), for an experimental study of the expansion of the triad.

away a member may help resolve one issue involved in the central hypothesis; namely, does the supraindividual component, mentioned by Simmel, depend strictly and unconditionally upon the existence of three parties? Is the integrative faculty of the threesome lost upon the withdrawal of a member, or is it somehow retained? Does a system, which possesses faculties for handling conflict, and whose members have experienced and participated in successful reintegration, automatically lose this ability when the necessary element for the creation of the faculties disappears? Or do members somehow operate as if the third element were present, thereby retaining its function as part of the culture of the pair? To what extent and under what conditions is there irreversibility of these processes? Does number determine the matter, or does the life-history of the group determine it?

Moreover, upon the departure of a member, we may ask how the organization of the initial triad affects the relationship between the two who remain. How do the affective, behavioral, and cognitive aspects of their relationship change? In what sorts of triads is integrative capacity lost, in what sorts is it retained? Finally, under increasing external demands, how do the curves of these remaining pairs compare with those which have not had a third member? Control groups for this project would consist simply of dyads and triads in which no change in membership occurs. In conclusion, it should be noted that the simple expedient of adding and subtracting members to clarify the dynamics of very small groups amounts to an important extension of Simmel's treatment, for he works to a great extent on the implicit assumption that groups increase but do not decrease in size—an assumption which probably biased his appreciation of the role of numbers in the process and organization of groups.

COMMENT

It is likely that the results of modern investigation of these matters will have been anticipated by Simmel, for it is his habit, after posing a concept or a proposition, to illustrate its feasibility with one example, its limitations with another, its general application with still others, and its antithesis by a final example, until it is fully circumscribed. As Hughes notes, he is tentative.[37] Habitually, he anticipates both negative and positive results. The seductive power of this habit of learning and of teaching is attested to by his early influence on American sociology. Yet students of science have come to recognize that a proposition, even though artfully suspended by positive and negative illustrations, is a long way from one about which one can make a probability statement. The task—the laborious task, indeed—of arriving at these probabilities, Simmel leaves to his students.

Though the purpose of this paper is to suggest several steps that might be taken in this direction, certain of Simmel's propositions are selected, rather than others, because they are of strategic importance to the development of social science. Within immediate social relations he observed configurations, and changes in configurations, of libidinal, communicative, and power ties which seemed to possess an order and a form, which, if carefully abstracted, might serve as models for more complex systems. Transpositions from the micro- to the macro-system may in itself prove valuable, but to limit his contribution to this alone is to underestimate Simmel's intuition and to lead away, rather than toward, the significance of his strategy.

He invented a way—his formal model—for dealing with the interrelation of parts of complex systems. The total organization of these interrelations is the very property of systems which cannot be explained by use of analytical variables alone, however elaborate. Crystal formation is an analogous case in physical science, and, closer to home, is the social configuration we call the Oedipus situation—for which, as far as I am aware, no sociological theory can account. Freud's treatment of this problem gained its power precisely because he combined Simmel-like sociology with his own personality theory. Perhaps comparable strength will be lent to sociological analysis by combining theories based on analytical variables with configurational models on the order visualized but never fully developed by Simmel.

[37] *Conflict . . . , op. cit.*, p. 8.

# TWO

# REALISTIC AND NONREALISTIC CONFLICT

## LEWIS A. COSER

If the conflict is caused by an object, by the will to have or control something, by rage or revenge . . . it is qualified by the fact that, in principle, every end can be attained by more than one means. The desire for possession or subjugation, even for the annihilation of the enemy, can be satisfied through combinations and events other than fight. Where conflict is merely a means determined by a superior purpose, there is no reason to restrict or even avoid it, provided it can be replaced by other measures which have the same promise of success. Where, on the other hand, it is exclusively determined by subjective feelings, where there are inner energies which *can* be satisfied only through fight, its substitution by other means is impossible; it is its own purpose and content. . . .[1]

SIMMEL ASSERTS THAT conflicts occasioned by clashes of interests or clashes of personalities contain an element of limitation insofar as the struggle is only a means toward an end; if the desired result can be attained as well or better by other means, such other means may be employed. In such instances, conflict is only one of several functional alternatives.

There are cases, however, where the conflict arises exclusively from aggressive impulses which seek expression no matter what the object, where in the conflict the choice of object is purely accidental. In such cases no such limitations exist, since it is not the

From Lewis A. Coser, *The Functions of Social Conflict* (New York: The Free Press of Glencoe, Inc., 1956). Reprinted by permission of the publishers.

[1] Georg Simmel, *Conflict and the Web of Group Affiliations*, translated by Kurt H. Wolff and Reinhard Bendix (New York: The Free Press of Glencoe, Inc., 1955).

attainment of a result, but rather the acting out of aggressive energies which occasions the outbreak.

Implicit in this differentiation between conflict as a means and conflict as an end in itself is a criterion by which to distinguish between *realistic* and *nonrealistic* conflict. Conflicts which arise from frustration of specific demands within the relationship and from estimates of gains of the participants, and which are directed at the presumed frustrating object, can be called *realistic conflicts,* insofar as they are means toward a specific result. *Nonrealistic conflicts,* on the other hand, although still involving interaction between two or more persons, are not occasioned by the rival ends of the antagonists, but by the need for tension release of at least one of them. In this case the choice of antagonists depends on determinants not directly related to a contentious issue and is not oriented toward the attainment of specific results.

Else Frenkel-Brunswick, discussing the "ethnocentric personality," makes precisely this point when she writes: "Even his hate is mobile and can be directed from one object to another." [2] John Dewey's dictum, "men do not shoot because targets exist, but they set up targets in order that throwing and shooting may be more effective and significant," [3] applies to this type of nonrealistic conflict.

Thus anti-Semitism, except where it is caused by conflicts of interests or values between the Jewish and other groups or individuals, will be called *nonrealistic* insofar as it is primarily a response to frustrations in which the object appears suitable for a release of aggressiveness. Whether this object be Jews, Negroes, or some other group is of secondary importance to the aggressor. [4]

Nonrealistic conflict, occasioned by the need for release of aggressive tension in one or more of the interacting persons, is less "stable" than realistic conflict. The underlying aggressiveness can more

[2] Else Frenkel-Brunswick, "Interaction of Psychological and Sociological Factors in Political Behavior," *American Political Science Review,* XLVI (1952), 63.

[3] John Dewey, *Human Nature and Conduct* (New York: Modern Library Inc.), p. 226.

[4] The choice of objects is random on the psychological level, yet not random on the cultural and structural level, since suitability as a target for tension release depends on a number of structural and cultural factors. For a discussion of the large body of work which has been done in the field of object choice for prejudiced reactions, see Robin Williams, *The Reduction of Intergroup Tensions, Social Science Research Council Bulletin No. 57.*

easily be led into other channels, precisely because it is not directly bound to the object, which has become a target by "situational accident." It is likely to manifest itself in different ways if the particular object is no longer available.

Realistic conflict, on the other hand, will cease if the actor can find equally satisfying alternative ways to achieve his end.[5] In realistic conflict, there exist *functional alternatives as to means.* Means other than conflict, depending on assessments of their efficacy, are always potentially available to the participants. In addition, it should be noted that in realistic conflicts there are also possibilities of choice between various forms of contention, such choice depending similarly on an assessment of their instrumental adequacy. In nonrealistic conflict, on the other hand, there exist only *functional alternatives as to objects.*

A distinction along these lines should help to avoid the fallacy of trying to explain the social phenomena of realistic conflict entirely in terms of "tension release." For example, a worker engaged in strike activity in order to increase his wages, his status, or the power of his union, and one who releases aggression against the boss because he perceives him as an Oedipal figure, are dissimilar social types. Displaced father hatred may attach itself to any suitable object—boss, policeman, or staff sergeant. The economic fight of workers against the boss, on the other hand, is based on their particular positions and roles in the economic and political

[5] The distinction which is proposed here is roughly similar to that between instrumental and expressive behavior which informs many aesthetic theories. Cf., for example, John Dewey's *Art as Experience* (New York: Minton, Balch & Co., 1935). Some modern psychologists have employed it also. Thus in his article, "The Expressive Component of Personality" (*Psychological Review,* LVI [1949], 261-72), A. H. Maslow distinguishes between coping—i.e., the instrumental and purposive—on the one hand, and the expressive—i.e., noninstrumental components—of behavior—on the other. Coping behavior "comes into existence to get something done . . . it implies a reference to something beyond it; it is not self-contained." Expressive behavior, however, "simply mirrors, reflects, signifies, or expresses some state of the organism. Indeed, it most often is part of that state."

Similarly, Henry A. Murray ("Toward a Classification of Interaction," in Parsons and Shils, *Toward a General Theory of Action, op. cit.,* pp. 445 ff.) distinguishes between effect needs and activity needs. An activity need is "a disposition to engage in a certain type of activity for its own sake. . . . The satisfaction is contemporary with the activity itself . . . and it can be distinguished from the contentment that follows some achieved effect."

system. They can choose to give up the conflict and reach accommodation if it seems opportune to do so; they can also choose means of carrying it out other than strikes, such as collective bargaining, negotiations, slowdowns, and so on.

Antagonistic action on the part of labor against management, or vice versa, can be said to be realistic insofar as it is a means for obtaining results (higher status, more power, greater economic returns); if the aim of labor or management is the achievement of these results and not the mere expression of diffuse hostilities, such conflict is less likely to take place whenever alternative means will help to attain the goal.

Such a distinction might serve to inform discussions of social control and social deviance. A social deviant need not be "irrational," or devoid of reality orientation, as much theorizing has tacitly assumed. The deviant behavior which Merton analyzes in "Social Structure and Anomie," [6] insofar as it represents efforts to reach culturally prescribed goals through culturally tabooed means, would constitute one of the variants of realistic struggle. If the type of deviants involved here should find at their disposal legitimate means to attain the same goal, they are less likely to engage in deviant behavior. Deviance, in this case, is more nearly instrumental than expressive. Other types of deviance, however, may serve to release tension accumulated during the socialization process and through frustration and deprivations in adult roles. In these cases the deviant values the aggressive behavior in itself; the object against which the act is directed is of secondary import. Fulfillment of the tensional need is primary, and hence the act does not serve as a means to the attainment of a specific result. In such cases, there is less likely to be a weighing of peaceful against aggressive means, since it is precisely in the aggressive means and not in the result that satisfaction is sought.[7]

[6] Merton, *Social Theory and Social Structure* (New York: The Free Press of Glencoe, Inc., 1949), pp. 125-49.

[7] Clyde Kuckhohn's "Group Tensions" (Bryson, Finkelstein, and MacIver [eds.], *Approaches to National Unity* [New York: Harper & Row, Publishers, 1945]), incidentally one of the very few works in which the distinction between realistic and nonrealistic conflicts is clearly made, supplies one of the most lucid general descriptions of the sources of nonrealistic conflict. Cf. Gordon Allport's discus-

Failure to make the proposed distinction accounts for much of the confusion in current research on "tensions" and "aggression." [8] Knowledge gained from the study of nonrealistic conflict is being applied to the field of international relations, overlooking the fact that conflicts in this field are primarily realistic conflicts of power, interests, or values and that the nonrealistic elements which may be intermingled in the struggle are contingent and play, at best, a reinforcing role.[9] As Alvin Johnson has said:

> It is commonly assumed that antipathies between people . . . have played a large part in the causation of war. History offers singularly little evidence upon which such a view can be based. . . . Such antipathies . . . appear rather to be the result than a cause of war.[10]

The psychologist who studies displacement mechanisms is rightly concerned primarily with the personality of the prejudiced individual, while the target of the aggressive drive concerns him only incidentally. But in the study of a conflict situation in which the *interaction* is of major concern, the sociologist must investigate the conflict relationship and the exclusive values or divergent interests

---

sion of realistic and nonrealistic conflict in *The Nature of Prejudice* (Cambridge: Addison-Wesley Press, 1954), especially pp. 229-33.

See also Talcott Parsons' article, "Some Primary Sources and Patterns of Aggression in the Social Structure of the Western World" (*Essays in Sociological Theory* [New York: The Free Press of Glencoe, Inc., 1949], pp. 251-74) for an effort to trace more specifically some of the sources of nonrealistic conflict in the institutional structure of Western societies.

[8] See, e.g., Otto Klineberg, *Tensions Affecting International Understanding*, *Bulletin No. 62* (New York: SSRC, 1950), and Stuart Chase, *Roads to Agreement* (New York: Harper & Row, Publishers, 1951).

[9] As Reinhold Niebuhr has cogently argued: "Educators . . . underestimate the conflict of interest in political and economic relations, and attribute to disinterested ignorance what ought usually to be attributed to interested intelligence." (*Moral Man and Immoral Society* [New York: Charles Scribner's Sons, 1932], p. 215.)

[10] *Encyclopaedia of the Social Sciences*, XV, pp. 336-37.

Theodore Abel, in a study of twenty-five major wars, states that he found "in no case the decision [to use war] precipitated by emotional tension, sentimentality, crowd behavior, or other irrational motivations." ("The Element of Decision in the Pattern of War," *American Sociological Review*, VI [1941], p. 855.)

Cf. also Stanislaw Andrzejewski, *Military Organization and Society* (London: Routledge & Kegan Paul, Ltd., 1954).

which the contenders pursue.[11] There is no justification for *a priori* regarding claims in a conflict situation as equivalent to the statement that "the center of the earth is made of jam."[12] Thus a sociological study of international politics, although it may legitimately concern itself with tensions arising from various frustrations within national social systems, will not accomplish its main purpose unless it analyzes the realistic conflicts over scarce power around which the patterns of alliance and antagonisms form.

Similarly, the studies in industrial sociology inspired by Elton Mayo show no recognition of the existence of realistic conflict or of its functions. Behavior which is the outcome of a conflict situation is almost exclusively dealt with as nonrealistic behavior. They counterpose a logic of facts, "the logic of cost and the logic of efficiency" (i.e., "facts" which aim at beneficial results for management) to "the logic of sentiments," thus depriving the workers' claims of their realistic basis. "The implication that emerges, whether intended or not, is that managers are guided by a logic of reason, whereas workers are largely creatures of feelings and emotions."[13] The emphasis on "sentiments" obscures the existence of realistic conflict. Indeed, these studies show a peculiar lack of sensitivity to struggles over power or pecuniary gains that arise in the factory.

With the possibility of realistic conflict ruled out, the managerial sociologists are naturally led to "wonder what kind of man it must be who can get such an idea into his head" and, instead of directing their attention to the investigation of the conflict situation, they look for "therapeutic measures." Committed to the view that the

[11] Jessie Bernard is one of the very few sociologists who have attacked the psychologistic interpretation of conflict. Cf. "The Conceptualization of Intergroup Relations with Special Reference to Conflict," *Social Forces*, XXIX (1951), 243-51.

[12] Reference is here made to Freud's distinction between statements which are plausible and those which are nonsensical. If "a person comes along who seriously asserts that the center of the earth is made of jam," the result will be "a diversion of our interests; instead of their being directed on to the investigation itself, as to whether the interior of the earth is really made of jam or not, we shall wonder what kind of man it must be who can get such an idea into his head . . . ." (*New Introductory Lectures on Psychoanalysis* [New York: W. W. Norton & Company, Inc., 1933], pp. 48-49.)

[13] Delbert C. Miller and William H. Form, *Industrial Sociology* (New York: Harper & Row, Publishers, 1951), p. 79.

source of conflict is to be found in sentiments which distort relations rather than in the nature of these social relations themselves, they see all conflict as "social disease" and the lack of conflict as "social health." [14] Their center of attention is neither the source of frustration nor the issue at stake, but the effect of frustration on the individual. In the words of Dale Carnegie, they attempt "to make the other man happy about the thing you suggest" by directing feelings of hostility into "safe" channels.[15] Thus Roethlisberger and Dickson can write with admirable frankness about the counseling system: "This kind of nonauthoritative agency serves to control and direct those human processes within the industrial structure which are not adequately controlled by other agencies of management." [16]

The distinction between realistic and nonrealistic conflict involves a conceptual abstraction from concrete reality in which the two types actually may be merged. However, as Max Weber has pointed out, "the construction of a purely rational course of action . . . serves the sociologist as a type. . . . By comparison with this it is possible to understand the ways in which actual action is influenced by irrational factors of all sorts . . . in that they account for the deviation from the line of conduct which would be expected on the hypothesis that the action was purely rational." [17]

Realistic conflict situations may be accompanied, especially where there are no adequate provisions for the carrying out of the struggle,

[14] Cf. Reinhard Bendix and Lloyd Fisher, "The Perspectives of Elton Mayo," *Review of Economics and Statistics*, XXXI (1949), 312-19.

[15] This explains the total neglect of unions in the original Mayo studies; see Harold L. Sheppard, "The Treatment of Unionism in 'Managerial Sociology,' " *American Sociological Review*, XIV (1949), 310-13. See also Robert Sorensen, "The Concept of Conflict in Industrial Sociology," *Social Forces*, XXIX (1951), 263-67, and Arthur Kornhauser *et al.*, *Industrial Conflict* (New York: McGraw-Hill Book Company, Inc., 1954), especially the paper by Clark Kerr and Abraham Siegel.

[16] Roethlisberger and Dickson, *Management and the Worker* (Cambridge, Mass.: Harvard University Press, 1939), p. 601. See also the critical evaluation of the Hawthorne Counseling Program by Jeanne L. and Harold L. Wilensky, "Personnel Counseling: The Hawthorne Case," *American Journal of Sociology*, LVII (1951), 365 ff.

[17] Max Weber, *The Theory of Social and Economic Organization*, translated by Talcott Parsons and A. M. Henderson (New York: Oxford University Press, Inc., 1947), p. 92.

by unrealistic sentiments which are deflected from their source. In concrete social reality an admixture of both "pure" types will be found. Talcott Parsons expressed this very well in his description of the scapegoat mechanism:

> Since it would be dangerous and wrong to freely express overt antagonism toward the members of the in-group, it is often psychologically easier to "displace" the affect onto an out-group in relation to which there *already exists*[18] some basis of antagonism. Scapegoating thus rarely appears without *some*[19] "reasonable" basis of antagonism in that there is a real conflict of ideals or interests.[20]

In other words, one of the sources of unrealistic admixtures in realistic conflicts lies in institutions which define the free expression of overt antagonism as "dangerous and wrong."

The term *realistic conflict* does not necessarily imply that the means adopted are actually adequate for reaching the end in view; the means may merely seem to be adequate to the participants, if only for the reason that they are culturally approved. Workers who go on strike to force the exclusion from the shop of Negro fellow workers in order to maintain their wage rates are engaged in realistic conflict. But (and this is the essence of Simmel's proposition) if the situation is so changed that other means prove more rewarding with regard to wage rates, the workers are more likely to refrain from discriminatory action. Should they, however, maintain the discriminatory practice although other more effective means to the same end are available, it can be provisionally supposed that nonrealistic elements, such as prejudice, are being expressed in the conflict.[21]

Perhaps enough has been said to clarify the reasons for distinguishing between realistic and nonrealistic types of conflict.

[18] Emphasis mine—L.C.
[19] Emphasis in the original.
[20] Talcott Parsons, *Religious Perspectives of College Teaching in Sociology and Social Psychology* (New Haven: The Edward W. Hagen Foundation, n.d.), p. 40.
[21] The distinction here proposed is similar to one proposed by Merton in a paper on "Discrimination and the American Creed," in R. M. MacIver (ed.), *Discrimination and National Welfare* (New York: Harper & Row, Publishers, 1948). Cf. also T. W. Adorno *et al.*, *The Authoritarian Personality* (New York: Harper & Row, Publishers, 1950).

Each social system contains sources of realistic conflict insofar as people raise conflicting claims to scarce status, power, and resources, and adhere to conflicting values. The allocation of status, power, and resources, though governed by norms and role allocation systems, will continue to be an object of contention to some degree. Realistic conflicts arise when men clash in the pursuit of claims based on frustration of demands and expectancies of gains.

Nonrealistic conflicts arise from deprivations and frustrations stemming from the socialization process and from later adult role obligations, or they result, as we have seen in the previous proposition, from a conversion of originally realistic antagonism which was disallowed expression. Whereas the first type of conflict takes place with the frustrating agents themselves in expectation of attaining specific results, the second type consists of a release of tension in aggressive action directed against shifting objects. The first type of conflict is viewed by the participants as a means toward the achievement of realistic ends, a means which might be abandoned if other means appear to be more effective for reaching the same end. The second leaves no such choice, since satisfaction is derived from the aggressive act itself. . . .

BIBLIOGRAPHY

# SIMMEL'S BOOKS IN GERMAN AND ENGLISH

## SIMMEL'S BOOKS IN GERMAN

1881    *Das Wesen der Materie nach Kants physischer Monadologie.* Berlin: Druck der Norddeutschen Buchdruckerei, 1881.

1890    *Über sociale Differenzierung. Sociologische und psychologische Untersuchungen.* Leipzig: Duncker und Humblot, 1890.

1892    *Die Probleme der Geschichtsphilosophie. Eine erkenntnistheoretische Studie.* Leipzig: Duncker und Humblot, 1892.

1892-93    *Einleitung in die Moralwissenschaft. Eine Kritik der ethischen Grundbegriffe.* Berlin: Hertz (Besser), Vol. I, 1892, Vol. II, 1893.

1900    *Philosophie des Geldes.* Leipzig: Duncker und Humblot, 1900.

1904    *Kant. Sechzehn Vorlesungen gehalten an der Berliner Universität.* Leipzig: Duncker und Humblot, 1904.

1905    *Philosophie der Mode.* Berlin: Pan-Verlag, 1905.

1906 (a) *Kant und Goethe.* Berlin: Marquardt, 1906.

     (b) *Die Religion.* Frankfurt am Main: Rütten und Loening, 1906.

1907    *Schopenhauer und Nietzsche: Ein Vortragszyklus.* Leipzig: Duncker und Humblot, 1907.

1908    *Soziologie: Untersuchungen über die Formen der Vergesellschaftung.* Leipzig: Duncker und Humblot, 1908.

1910    *Hauptprobleme der Philosophie.* Leipzig: Göschen, 1910.

1911    *Philosophische Kultur: Gesammelte Essays.* Leipzig: Kröner, 1911.

1913    *Goethe.* Leipzig: Klinkhardt und Biermann, 1913.

1914    *Deutschlands innere Wandlung.* Strasbourg: Trübner, 1914.

1916    (a) *Das Problem der historischen Zeit.* Berlin: Reuther und Reichard, 1916.

(b) *Rembrandt. Ein kunstphilosophischer Versuch.* Leipzig: Wolff, 1916.

1917    (a) *Grundfragen der Soziologie (Individuum und Gesellschaft).* Berlin and Leipzig: de Gruyter, 1917.

(b) *Der Krieg und die geistigen Entscheidungen: Reden und Aufsätze.* Munich and Leipzig: Duncker und Humblot, 1917.

1918    (a) *Der Konflikt der modernen Kultur: Ein Vortrag.* Munich and Leipzig: Duncker und Humblot, 1918.

(b) *Lebensanschauung: Vier metaphysische Kapitel.* Munich and Leipzig: Duncker und Humblot, 1918.

(c) *Vom Wesen des historischen Verstehens.* Berlin: Mittler, 1918.

(*Published Posthumously*)

1922    (a) *Zur Philosophie der Kunst: Philosophische und kunstphilosophische Aufsätze,* Gertrud Simmel (ed.). Potsdam: Kiepenheuer, 1922.

(b) *Schulpädagogik. Vorlesungen,* Karl Hauter (ed.). Osterwieck/ Harz: Zickfeldt, 1922.

1923    *Fragmente und Aufsätze aus dem Nachlass und Veröffentlichungen der letzten Jahre,* Gertrud Kantorowicz (ed.). Munich: Drei Masken Verlag, 1923.

1957    *Brücke und Tür: Essays des Philosophen zur Geschichte, Religion, Kunst, und Gesellschaft,* Michael Landmann and Margarete Susman (eds.). Stuttgart: Koehler, 1957.

SIMMEL'S BOOKS IN ENGLISH

1950    *The Sociology of Georg Simmel,* translated and edited by Kurt H. Wolff. New York: The Free Press of Glencoe, Inc.

1955    *Conflict and The Web of Group-Affiliation,* translated by Kurt H. Wolff and Reinhard Bendix, with a foreword by Everett C. Hughes. New York: The Free Press of Glencoe, Inc.

1959    *Sociology of Religion,* translated by Curt Rosenthal. New York: The Wisdom Library, a Division of Philosophical Library, Inc.

For fuller bibliographies of writings by and on Simmel see the following:

1. Kurt H. Wolff (ed.), *Georg Simmel, 1858-1918.* Columbus, Ohio: The Ohio State University Press, 1959.

2. *The Sociology of Georg Simmel,* cited above.

3. Erich Rosenthal and Kurt Oberlaender, "Books, Papers and Essays by Georg Simmel," *American Journal of Sociology,* LI (1945), 238-47.

# CONTRIBUTORS

LEWIS A. COSER studied at the Sorbonne and at Columbia University, from which he received his Ph.D. in 1954. He has taught at the University of Chicago and at the University of California (Berkeley). He is now Professor of Sociology at Brandeis University. A former Vice President and currently President of the Eastern Sociological Society, he is the author of a number of volumes, including *The Functions of Social Conflict; Sociological Theory* (with Bernard Rosenberg); *Sociology through Literature;* and *The American Communist Party: A Critical History* (with Irving Howe). He has written extensively for the scholarly journals, as well as for *Commentary* and *The Partisan Review*. He is an editor of *Dissent* magazine.

ÉMILE DURKHEIM, greatest of the French sociologists, ranks next to Max Weber in his influence on modern social science. His basic work in the methodology of the social sciences, and his volumes on *Suicide* and *The Elementary Forms of the Religious Life* are among the few classics of sociology.

FERDINAND TÖNNIES was the dean of German sociology. His writings have deeply influenced subsequent generations of German sociologists from Max Weber to Karl Mannheim. His best known work, *Gemeinschaft und Gesellschaft,* is available in English translation as *Community and Society* (1957).

LEOPOLD VON WIESE taught for many years at the University of Cologne. One of the founders of the German Sociological Society, he helped reconstitute it after the Nazi period. He is best known as the founder of a system of formal sociology which was influenced by Georg Simmel's pioneering venture. He has had considerable influence in the United States as well as in his native Germany. He began publishing in 1906 and continues to be a productive scholar.

CÉLESTIN BOUGLÉ was deeply influenced by Durkheim's system of sociology but interpreted it in his own characteristic fashion. He taught for many years at the École Normale and at the Sorbonne. His life work contains, besides fine scholarly studies such as his discussion of the structure of caste societies, a number of major works aiming at a defense of democratic principles.

ALFRED MAMELET, French philosopher.

F. H. TENBRUCK, a young German sociologist who spent a number of years teaching in the United States, now holds a chair in sociology at the University of Frankfort.

183

DONALD N. LEVINE is a young American sociologist now teaching at the University of Chicago. His major interest in recent years has been in the social structure of Ethiopian society; he has done extensive research in Ethiopia and has started a series of publications on it.

RUDOLF HEBERLE was deeply influenced by Ferdinand Tönnies. His major interests are demography, the sociology of politics, and the interrelations between geographic and social phenomena. His *From Democracy to Nazism* (1945), a study of the rise of the Nazi movement in Schleswig-Holstein, has become a minor classic. His *Social Movements: An Introduction to Political Sociology* (1951) has also had considerable influence. He taught for many years at Louisiana State University, where he recently became professor emeritus.

RUDOLPH H. WEINGARTNER served as an instructor in Philosophy at Columbia University, was a fellow of the Institute for Philosophical Research, San Francisco, and is now a member of the faculty of San Francisco State College.

ALBERT SALOMON taught for many years at the New School of Social Research, where he is now emeritus. He studied under Simmel and Weber in Berlin and Heidelberg. He has written extensively on the major figures in German sociology, on the predecessors and founders of sociology from Bodin to Comte, and on the sociology of literature. His *Tyranny of Progress* (1955) has been widely discussed.

RAYMOND ARON, the distinguished French sociologist, holds a chair of sociology at the Sorbonne. Several of his numerous works, such as *The Opium of the Intellectuals,* and several volumes on the sociology of war, on international affairs, and on the philosophy of history, are available in English.

PITIRIM SOROKIN is one of the most outspoken of the critics of contemporary society. He is currently on the faculty of Harvard University, where he has been since 1930. He is the director of the Research Center in Creative Altruism and the author of numerous books, including *Social Philosophy of an Age of Crisis* (1950), *Social and Cultural Dynamics* (1962), *The American Sex Revolution* (1956), and *Crisis of Our Age: The Social and Cultural Outlook.*

THEODORE M. MILLS, a young American sociologist, was trained at Harvard University where he was influenced by Robert Bales' approach to the study of small experimental groups. He now teaches at Yale and devotes most of his scholarly work to the study of small groups. Among his publications is *Group Transformation: An Analysis of a Learning Group* (1964).